REGISTER FOR YOUR BOOK BONUSES AT:

YouHaveTheKeysNowDrive.com/resources

Praise for You Have the Keys, Now Drive

"You Have the Keys, Now Drive" helped me get unstuck when I felt stuck in the mud spinning my wheels in a job I had lost passion for. Deep down inside we often know the things that need to ultimately change in our lives but it's a bigger challenge figuring out how to make the change or drawing up the courage to make it happen. Danny's book was exactly the inspiration at exactly the right time. After reading the book, underlining almost everything and doing the exercises, I realized it was time to leave a good job which no longer brought me the joy and satisfaction it once did. I've since found the courage to leave and pursue a slightly different direction which has always intrigued me and I couldn't be happier about it. It's also challenged me to realistically re-examine other areas of my life that have been overlooked.

It's recommended reading for everyone who may find themselves at a crossroads."

Margot Daley, TV Producer

"If you're determined to change your life and contemplating where to start, Danny Stone's "You Have the Keys, Now Drive" can help. Using personal anecdotes and tools, Danny designed his book to help you get unstuck and focus on what you can do to lead a happier life and achieve your goals, both personally and professionally. You Have the Keys, Now Drive is worth the read for anyone committed to creating a roadmap for a better life."

Nadine Mauricette, Entrepreneur

"I'm far from an avid reader, in fact I rarely read books, however I am so glad I purchased this book. Danny is a master at providing real stories of struggle and triumph in a way that uncovers real keys to success and happiness. He lays out a step-by-step strategy to show people how to build confidence and achieve their goals. I love the "try this" at the end of the chapters. I dove in and did the activities and my life began to shift in a big way. I now have much more confidence and I am on my way to achieving a HUGE goal that I have struggled with for years."

Brian Anderson, Consulting Professional

You Have the Keys, Now Drive

5 Keys and 5 Habits to Personal Change

Danny Stone

You Have the Keys, Now Drive

Mentions of specific companies, organizations, or authorities in this book do not imply endorsement by the author or publisher, nor does the mention of specific companies, organizations or authorities imply that they endorse this book, the author or publisher.

Copyright © 2018 Danny Stone. All rights reserved.

Personify Consulting Publishing

All rights reserved. This book or any portion thereof may not be reproduced or used in any manner whatsoever without the written consent of the author.

First Printing: 2014
Second Printing: 2018
ISBN-13: 978-0-9936113-2-2

Personify Consulting Publishing
Toronto, Ontario, Canada

First Edition February 2014
Second Edition July 2018

Printed in Canada

www.youhavethekeysnowdrive.com

Editing: Nancy Davis
Book Cover: Trudy Stone

CONTENTS

Dedication	vii
Special Invitation	ix
A Note to You, the Reader	xi
Introduction	1

Part I: The Five Keys to Personal Change

1	First Key: Develop a Vision	9
2	Second Key: Get to Know You	21
3	Third Key: Permission to Fail	29
4	Fourth Key: Follow Your Curiosity	37
5	Fifth Key: Your Life Support Network	53

Part II: The Five Habits to Personal Change

6	First Habit: Establish a Morning Ritual	65
7	Second Habit: Develop a Bedtime Routine	79
8	Third Habit: Get Going on Your Goals	85

9	Fourth Habit: Mind Your Fitness and Spirit	99
10	Fifth Habit: Be of Service to Others	107

Conclusion   113

Special Invitation (If you missed it the first time!)   119

About the Author   121

Hire Danny to Speak!   123

DEDICATION

First and foremost, this book is dedicated to Trudy Stone. Your passion to explore the world around you and your compassion for others truly inspire me to do the same.

To my family, especially my mother Marcia, sister Tamara, and brother MJ. Your belief in me has driven me to do things that I did not know I could achieve.

Last but certainly not least, a very special dedication to my late grandparents, Monica and Lloyd Stone. Thank you for instilling the values, confidence, and work ethic in me that gives me the courage to achieve my goals rather than settle, and for nurturing my desire to step outside of my comfort zone.

SPECIAL INVITATION FOR YOU

Driver of Your Destiny Community

Readers, fans, and followers of "You Have the Keys, Now Drive" and my work are extraordinary people committed to waking up ready for personal change and ready to unlock their true potential. Knowing that there are many individuals ready to make a shift in their lives that don't have the tools or resources to do so, inspired me to create the Driver of Your Destiny community. The community is a place for you to connect, share ideas, get guidance and support, discuss the book, find accountability partners, and motivate others.

Sign up for the free community on Facebook at
www.facebook.com/groups/driverofyourdestiny

Here you will connect with like-minded individuals who are committed to personal change and personal growth. You can share your keys to personal change stories, discuss how you are building your confidence, and share how your new habits are helping you achieve your biggest goals.

I will be moderating the community, regularly checking in and commenting. I would love to hear from you on social media.

My name is **@iamDannyStone** on Instagram, Twitter, Facebook, Pinterest, and YouTube. Please feel free to comment, like and direct message me. I read every comment and do my absolute best to personally respond. Looking forward to seeing you in the community and on social media!

Go to www.facebook.com/groups/driverofyourdestiny

A NOTE TO YOU, THE READER

Congratulations on picking up this book, Should you choose to read it your life MAY change in a big way. There are activities that you can try along the way and if you do them things will be different in a positive way (of course I make no guarantees, I don't personally know you, your life, or your mindset). However, what I do know is that if you choose to change and take the massive actions that I suggest in this book, it is highly possible you will unlock your own personal change. I know because what is written in this book has already changed countless lives for the better, from everyday people like you and me to people we might see as highly successful. I have studied personal change, success, and happiness for years, I have coached hundreds of people and learned from my mentors and I share what I have learned with you in this book.

I first released this book in 2014 to help people take control of their lives, increase their self-confidence, and build powerful, positive habits to move them towards living the life they want. Little did I know it would impact so many people. The response has been positively overwhelming. I have been humbled and blessed that my book has resonated with people around the globe and amazed at how my words and actions have motivated others to light up their lives and take action.

In this revised second edition of *"You Have the Keys, Now Drive,"* I have added more insights, learning, and teachings that I have learned since publishing the book in 2014. I have also added essential habits that I think will help you get closer to having the success, happiness and fulfillment that you are seeking. Besides expanding on the core habits that I wrote about in the first edition, I share learning on how the importance of a proper amount of sleep and a bedtime routine sets you up for major success in the days, weeks, months, and years ahead.

Since writing this book, many audience members, coaching clients, family, friends, and social media followers have shared their difficulties with setting and achieving their goals. As a result, I have developed a simple and powerful goal-setting tool to help you crush your goals. In the tool, I share never-before secrets of highly successful people which help them consistently set and achieve their bold- est goals. In my research, of combing through interviews and reading books of highly successful people, I developed a goal-setting strategy. I share this step-by-step strategy with you in this revised edition.

I truly want you to live your amazing life. I want you to unlock your greatness.

I love what Will Smith says about greatness. He says,

"Greatness is not this wonderful, esoteric, elusive, god-like feature that only the special among us will ever taste, it's something that truly exists in all of us."

This is the absolute truth! Please understand that no matter what challenges you are facing, how difficult the road you are traveling appears to be, or regardless of the successes that you have already had in your life; you can soar higher. You have greatness within you, you just have to find it and let it out.

Your life has meaning and purpose. You may not know it right now or you may be on your path to living your purpose. Either way, the road to get there is both simple and complicated at the same time because nothing worth achieving is easy.

You must learn from your past and take heed of the lessons you have learned along the way. Also, understand that your keys to success and happiness lie within you. Developing powerful, positive, consistent habits will change your life and you will unlock the greatness within you. In this book, I teach you how to change your habits by taking small steps that lead to massive action. We are going to work together to help you gain clarity, figure out what you really want and take action to achieve your goals. You deserve more. You deserve to be the best version of yourself. Let's work together to build the life you want.

INTRODUCTION

> *"Your beliefs become your thoughts, your thoughts become your words, your words become your actions, your actions become your habits, your habits become your values, your values become your destiny"*
>
> –Mahatma Gandhi

ARE YOU A DRIVER OF YOUR DESTINY OR A PASSENGER IN YOUR PURPOSE?

Are you a driver or a passenger of your own life?

Do you take control of your life or do you wait for things to happen?

These are the questions that you must ask yourself if you want to live a full life. If you want to find your true gift or talent and use it to uplift and enrich the lives of others, you must first understand where you are in your own life. At some point, you must get out of the passenger seat. You must undo your seatbelt, open the door, get out of the car, walk around to the driver's side, open the door and kick out the driver of your life. Tell fear, doubt, other people's opinions, all of the bad decisions you have made, any challenges that have held you back and all of your failures to get up out of the driver's seat because YOU are now the driver of your destiny not the passenger in your purpose.

In 2011, I was 40 pounds overweight. I was not eating healthy, and I was not feeling great about myself. Having been a former athlete who played university basketball, I had always been fit. Being overweight was a big deal for me because I had never been unfit in my life. Something had to change. My habits had to change, or rather, be replaced. Like most people, I knew I had to do something different but I was too comfortable. I knew it would be difficult to lose weight so I continued along the same path. I kept eating poorly and not exercising and when I thought about losing 40 pounds it seemed like it would take forever to lose the weight, so I did nothing to change my situation. It was like I was stuck in the mud. My life felt, heavy, sticky, I was weighed down, sluggish, and I couldn't seem to climb out of the mud. Growing up poor, my family couldn't always afford to eat healthily, we had to eat whatever my mother could afford, and that is where I began to form my eating habits. We had to eat whatever was on the table and my mom, being a single mom with three kids, often had to provide whatever she could. Back when I was overweight I made excuses to justify why I was overweight, "I don't have time to work out," "I can't afford to eat healthily," "It's too difficult to workout every day. I had all the good ones. It was easy for me to blame my weight gain on other things: my lack of nutritious meals growing up, no time to exercise, and everything else I just mentioned, however, life and situations are always about perspective.

I also remember going to my grandparents' house where they had a fruit and vegetable garden in the back yard. My grandparents immigrated to Canada from Jamaica back in the 1940s. In Jamaica, they grew up eating healthy food. They had mango and coconut trees, fresh meat from farmers, and their parents grew lots of fruits and vegetables as well. When I was young my mother would take me to visit my grandparents. I loved to pick fruits and vegetables from their garden. I would bring what I picked to my grandmother and together, we would cook up delicious, healthy meals. There were also times when my grandmother and I would take field trips to visit her best friend, Mrs. James. Mrs. James had a huge piece of land and a massive greenhouse. We would go there and get bags and bags of fruits and vegetables that my grandparents never grew in their small backyard garden.

Why am I telling you all of this? I am telling you because back when I was making excuses about my weight, I needed to change my perspective and change my actions. I had to stop justifying being overweight and blaming my past and find inspiration to move me into action.

One morning it all changed. I woke up like every other morning with no real plan, no vision, and no goals. I was tired of just existing. I'm not saying that I was suicidal, I wanted more out of life and I realized that my being overweight was a reflection of how I felt about myself and my life. I looked in the mirror and said "something has to change. I can't live like this. There has to be more in life than this. God, you must have a bigger plan for me." It was at that moment I realized that I had to replace my bad habits with healthier ones. I reminded myself that sports were a huge part of my life. I knew I had to get back to the energetic, confident, healthy person that I once was; that was my wake-up call. That was the day I decided to become a driver of my health, my life. I decided to replace my bad eating habits with healthier ones. I stopped making excuses and committed to exercising 3 days each week. I made a realistic plan to eat healthy 5 days a week and to go to the gym 3 days a week. I stuck with the plan until it became a routine, then a habit. Within eight weeks I had achieved my ideal weight. I regained my self-confidence, looked great in my clothes and had more energy. It happened because I changed my mindset from one of making excuses and feeling sorry for myself, to look at life from a new angle of knowing what I wanted and how I wanted to feel. Once I changed my mindset, I committed to taking small, consistent steps every day until I achieved my goal.

You see, when I was overweight, I was stuck. Not just stuck being overweight, but weighed down in so many other areas of my life as well. That is why I described it as being stuck in the mud. The mud was weighing me down and I felt like there was no way to crawl out, I realized that I had to pull myself out. I had to push myself to get up and do something different. I washed off the mud and moved on in my life. Maybe you can relate. Maybe there is something weighing you down, something holding you back in some area of your life. Maybe you need to crawl out of the mud, wash it off, and move on.

What does this mean for you? It means YOU can change your mindset and replace your habits. You have the ability to achieve your BIGGEST goals and dreams. You can accomplish things you never imagined possible if you understand the 5 Keys and 5 Habits you will about read in this book.

PART ONE - FIVE KEYS OF PERSONAL CHANGE

In the first part of this book, you will begin to prepare your mind to make a shift in your life. You will start to prepare yourself for personal change and you will learn the 5 Keys to help you make those changes. The Keys are principles and life lessons that are the foundation to help you build your best life and be your best self. Many of these Keys may be familiar to you, however, it is very important to truly understand what they mean for you and your personal journey. At the end of each chapter, you will find a TRY THIS section, something that you can try to make it more real and relevant for your life.

WHAT ARE THE KEYS?

The Keys to personal change are life lessons or principles to help you change your thoughts, actions, and behaviors. These Keys will prepare you to take massive action and replace the habits that are not serving you with new habits which will help you build the life you want. Some of the Keys will be reminders for you; things that you may have already incorporated into your life. Some may be new to you. Either way, these are principles that highly successful people live by. Many of my coaching clients, family, friends, and myself have embraced these Keys into our lives and have had tremendously positive results. From achieving goals we never thought possible, to developing more self-confidence, to starting successful businesses, to building amazing relationships, the Keys are principles we believe in and live every day

PART TWO - FIVE HABITS OF PERSONAL CHANGE

The second part of this book is all about action! You will get tips, stories, tools, and resources to help you take action right now. You will learn to replace the habits that are not serving you in a way that helps you build the life you want with habits that will help become the best version of yourself. The habits that you will learn have helped me, my coaching clients, and extremely successful people achieve success in many areas of their lives. They will help you do the same.

INTRODUCTION

WHAT ARE HABITS?

I am not going to get too sciencey here with you, (yes it is a word), but I need to explain to you what Habits really are and how they are formed.

A habit is a behavior that is repeated regularly and tends to occur subconsciously according to Wikipedia. It is something a person does without thinking. Examples of habits may include smoking, brushing your teeth every morning or, eating breakfast at the same time.

According to Dictionary.com, a habit is an acquired behavior pattern regularly followed until it has become almost involuntary.

In his book, *The Power of Habit*, author Charles Duhigg describes a habit as a three-step loop: the Cue, the Routine, the Reward. Duhigg describes the Cue is a trigger that tells the brain to go into automatic mode and which habit to use. The Routine is the physical, mental, or emotional action or aspect. Lastly, the Reward helps your brain figure out if the loop is worth remembering for the future.

What happens is that your brain becomes so used to the habit loop that it goes into automatic mode. It realizes that it doesn't have to work as hard because it remembers it has done this so many times before. The only way to break the loop and replace the habit is to consciously make an effort to replace the Routine. Duhigg also says that,

"*You can't extinguish a bad habit, you can only change it.*"

I agree with this quote. Based on my own personal experiences, Duhigg's quote really hit home for me. You cannot eliminate a habit that you have spent the majority of your life building and doing. It's ingrained in you. You can, however, replace the Routine.

Here's an example:

The Cue is that you are hungry.

The Routine is that you grab something quick and unhealthy out of the fridge to eat. The Reward is that you end your craving.

You will never stop the Cue. You will always be hungry a few times a day.

You will never change the reward which is ending the craving by eating.

What you can change is the ROUTINE. Instead of reaching for something fast, quick, and unhealthy, you can make a conscious effort and plan to cook something that will nourish your body. You could prepare healthy meals in advance, or purchase pre-made healthy meals, or other options.

The point is that you have to replace the Routine, the thing that you do, think or feel when the cue or trigger to do something arises. Start to think about your habits that are not serving you in a positive way. Begin thinking about your Cues, Routines, and Rewards.

HOW HABITS ARE FORMED

Again, I am not going to dive too deeply into how habits are formed, however, you should understand that your personal habits come from many different experiences and life events. Habits are formed from birth. They begin to develop as a child based on what you learn from parents, how you were raised, your environment, the schools you went to, the friends that you had, and other experiences.

An example would be when you are a young child, your parents establish your morning habit, they wake you up, tell you to use the washroom, wash your face, brush your teeth, and get dressed. Then you eat your breakfast, pack your lunch, grab your backpack, check your backpack to make sure your school work is in it, then go catch the school bus or get in the car. Your morning habits at that age are formed by your parents. Of course, as you become an adult, you adjust those habits for yourself. They may even change completely. However, in the beginning, your parents form your morning habits.

Later in life, your habits are formed by many factors such as your job, your relationships, your friends, your goals, your lifestyle, and many other influences. An important thing to remember about how your habits are formed is that they are formed over time through repetition. You have your Cues or triggers; you establish a Routine based on those triggers and you have an expected Reward based on the actions you take. Habits are not easily formed, nor are they easily replaced, however, it is possible to change your routine by changing your mindset. Once you make up your mind to change your routine, you can replace your habits.

THE 5 KEYS AND 5 HABITS TO PERSONAL CHANGE

I came up with the 5 Keys and 5 Habits to personal change based on my years of experience as a Career and Life Coach, my years of experience as a Personal Development Teacher, and everything I have learned from mentors and feedback from my readers.

In my research, I discovered that there are 5 Keys and 5 Habits that are essential in any personal change. I am talking about the kind of change that transforms one's life in a powerful, positive, and profound way. Whether you are feeling stuck or you are seeking more success and happiness in your life, the Keys and Habits will help you discover the current habits and patterns that are holding you back and keeping you stuck in the "mud" (a state of being stuck in some areas of your life). Most people who are stuck cannot see their situation from a different perspective because they do not understand that who they are and what they value is the catalyst for the decisions they make in life. Once people understand who they truly are and identify their values, passions, and life purpose it becomes the driving force behind how they live their lives. With these foundations, you will shift your perspective, set and achieve your goals, and have more success in your life; however, you choose to define success. And since success means different things to each one of us, it is important to stop and think about what success means to you.

THESE ARE THE 5 KEYS THAT YOU WILL LEARN THROUGHOUT THIS BOOK:

1. Develop a vision
2. Get to know yourself
3. Give yourself permission to fail
4. Follow your curiosity
5. Your life support team

THESE ARE THE 5 HABITS THAT YOU WILL LEARN THROUGHOUT THIS BOOK:

1. Establish morning ritual
2. Develop a bedtime routine
3. Get going on your goals
4. Mind your fitness and spirit
5. Be of service to others

Do you want more out of life? Then it is time to begin your journey and step into the life you want to live. Your new life begins now, but only if you choose to make it happen.

CHAPTER 1

FIRST KEY: DEVELOP A VISION

"Create the highest, grandest vision possible for your life, because you become what you believe."
—Oprah Winfrey

WHAT GOOD is seeing if you have no vision? I have played team sports my entire life. I have won championships and lost championships. On each journey to winning a championship, two things remained the same regardless of the team I was playing on and who the coach was: we always had a vision and a plan. Whether playing basketball in high school or university those two elements were the focus of all of the teams I have been part of. We had a bigger vision to win a championship each year and we had a plan to get us to that goal. Every day each team member would train in the gym, watch video footage of previous games, visualize themselves in-game situations and keep up with their studies. Some years we won championships and other years we were unsuccessful; however, even in failure, there were lessons. Not just lessons about winning and losing in sport, but winning and losing in life.

Using the idea of setting a vision for my goals in sports, I created a vision for what I wanted in my life. I decided what I wanted my life to look like in all areas that were important to me and I decided who I wanted to be and how I wanted to serve others. This vision connects with my values, passions, and purpose. When I created this vision for my life, everything changed for the better. I was more focused on what I wanted for me, I made better decisions, I had more confidence, and I surrounded myself with people who were supportive.

What is your vision for your life? What do you see for yourself over the next year, 10 years, or for the rest of your life? When you have a vision your life has more meaning and focus. You don't get sidetracked with other people's vision of YOUR life. You don't let challenges keep you down. You have more confidence, increased self-esteem, and you set bigger goals. Your life shifts in a very powerful way. It is your vision that acts as a north star, keeping you focused on being the best version of yourself and living a vibrant, curious, life.

In his book, *The School of Greatness*, Lewis Howes says this about vision...

> *"We focused first on creating a vision because it's the most important step to getting anywhere and achieving anything you want in any area of your life. But we also have to be clear about what a vision is. A vision is not just a dream. A powerful vision emerges when we couple our dreams with a set of clear goals. Without both, we are apt to wander in a clueless and purposeless fog, because a dream without goals is just a fantasy. And fantasies are the bad kind of visions – the hallucinogenic kind, not the real kind. Without a real vision, we lack identity. Having a real vision isn't just about clarifying what you want; It's about defining what and who you want to be"*

That's a very powerful statement, I completely agree with Lewis. If you want to live the life you truly desire, you need a vision. You need to know what you want in all areas of your life and how those areas all play together to help you create the best version of yourself. What do you want in your career? What does your best romantic relationship look like? What does it mean to be at peak health? These are questions you must ask yourself if you truly want personal change. When you know what you want in your life and you have goals your vision really comes alive.

Here is an example: Maybe there was a time when you started a new job. In starting that new job, maybe you had a bigger goal of what you wanted to achieve while you were working at that company. Either you wanted to learn as much as you could, then get promoted to a higher-level position or you had a goal to attain a certain salary. Regardless you had a bigger plan. The best way to get started with developing your vision is to sit down and think about what is important

FIRST KEY: DEVELOP A VISION

to you the most in your life. Is it your mental and physical health? Is it your family? Maybe it's financial freedom. What do you want in the most important areas of your life? Then you want to decide what you want in each area of your life. Think about what real success and happiness look like in all of those areas for you.

Let me describe three scenarios and break them down for you to understand this better. Let's use a career as an example. I will give you three scenarios, one or more may resonate with you.

SCENARIO 1:
You are looking for a new job and you do not have a preference for the kind of work you are seeking. You simply want to make more money. Your focus is to make a specific amount of money; you do not necessarily care about the job itself. You begin your job search by looking at any job that pays the salary you desire. After successfully going through the interview process you get the job. Congratulations you achieved your goal of finding a job paying the amount of money you are seeking. You start your new job. It is fine, but it's not your dream job or a job where you are utilizing your true talents, however, that paycheck is sweet. Within a few months to a year, you realize this is NOT the job for you. You are not passionate about the work, you are not stretching yourself mentally, and as a result, you are not producing your best work. Eventually, you quit your job because it is not satisfying and it doesn't bring you joy. Or even worse, you stick it out and coast for a few years until you finally get fired.

SCENARIO 2:
You are seeking a new job in your career field. You want a job where you are utilizing your skills and education. An ideal job would be something that pays you well, gives you a decent amount of vacation and doesn't require too much overtime. You begin the job search process and find an interesting role that matches your skills and education. You apply for the job, do well in the interview and get the job offer. In the beginning, over the first few months or years, it's good. You are using your skills and learning a little, but you are working more hours than expected

at times and the work has become repetitive. Eventually, you realize that you either don't want to be working for the company you are working for or you would rather work for another company. But you stay with the company. As time progresses, you get a promotion, that comes with a greater workload, however, you are not happy at the job. You begin to put in less effort because you are bored or your manager is not supportive enough or you simply don't want to be there. You continue going to work every day, wishing you were somewhere else, however, you do not look for other opportunities inside or outside of the company. Years go by, and you feel stuck in the job. You are not happy with the work you are doing. This continues for a few more years and you wake up one day and realize you have been at your job for 7 years and you have been unhappy in your career for the last 5 years.

SCENARIO 3:

You are seeking a new career opportunity, something that fits with your vision, passions, and where you are utilizing your talents and skills. It fits with your desire to serve others using your talents or gifts. You begin your search, being very specific about the organizations that you want to work for, you want to work for companies that have the same values as you. You are seeking specific roles that allow you to utilize your talents. You are seeking a place where you can continue to learn and grow your career. You find a company that is aligned with your vision and values and they have roles that you are completely passionate about. You apply for the role and you get a job offer. You accept it and begin working for the company. The work is exciting. You get to use your talents and your gifts. You have opportunities to learn and grow, and the people you are serving are getting amazing value. Your career progresses beyond any level you had imagined., your personal life is going great; your health and well-being are the best they have ever been, and you have more confidence than ever before. You feel so alive. You feel like this is what you have been missing in your life and you are extremely happy with where you are in your life.

    Of these three scenarios which one would you choose? Which one has been the norm for you?

FIRST KEY: DEVELOP A VISION

Most people would think the third scenario is not possible. They think that it is impossible to have this bigger vision for your career and actually make it a reality. This is where most people fail themselves. If you set low expectations and you lack a vision for your life, career, relationships, or finances, the best thing that will happen is that you will achieve your low expectations. Worse, you stumble through life with no purpose and no sense of how you can truly serve others. As a result, you end up giving up on yourself. Too many people are afraid to create a vision of a purpose-driven life for fear of failure. They think, "what's the point, I'll never be able to live that life." You cannot go through life with a loser's mentality. You cannot be a passenger in your life. Stop letting life happen, **make it what you want it to be.**

Create a vision for yourself. What do you see for yourself, your family, and the people that you want to serve?

I know some of you may be thinking, "that's great, but I need to make money; I don't have the luxury of waiting for my dream job or a role that is aligned with my vision." I agree. Life isn't a fairytale. Things often don't work out the way you want them to but that doesn't mean you shouldn't create a vision for your life. It means you should turn up your level of discipline to stay focused on what you really want. There are other ways that you can pursue your dream job. If you cannot land that amazing job at that amazing company that pays that amazing salary and allows you to pursue your passions or purpose; keep looking. Or, you can find other ways to use your talents and gifts to serve others. You can volunteer in your community, you can start a side-business, or you can find mentors who are doing what you want to do.

Once you set your vision for your life, you see possibilities, and in those possibilities is a journey to become the best version of yourself. When you become the best version of yourself, your life opens up, you get closer to finding real purpose and meaning and that is when you can take action to get what you want. You will become more resilient when things go wrong, and you will become more resourceful and find ways to make your vision a reality. You will wake up and go to bed knowing that you are meant to live the life you want. In some cases, you will set bigger goals and take action, and in other cases, you will just follow your curiosity and see where it leads you.

In writing this book, I vowed to be completely honest with you and with myself. In that honesty I will say this…without a vision for your life you may end up living in the middle. You may end up in jobs that are holding you back in your career, relationships that are unfulfilling and your life decisions will be made without a bigger meaning. That's what may happen. That is what DID happen to me until I set a vision for my life.

My want for you is to set a vision. To look at your life and ask yourself where you want more, where can you serve more, where can you grow more. Think about what true success and happiness look like in ALL areas of your life. What does success look like in your career, your health, your parenting, your finances, your romantic relationships, and your lifestyle?

Your goals and dreams are possible however, you have to see it for yourself first. Sit down and write out your vision for yourself. Look at the areas of your life and tell yourself what you want in your career or business, your relationships, as a parent, in your health, in your finances, and other areas of importance of your life. If you do this and you take action your life will open up like never before.

EXERCISE #1: WHEEL OF LIFE

The Wheel of Life fell into my lap many years ago. I cannot remember how I just remember coming across it somewhere and the activity really created more clarity in my life. The Wheel of Life is a tool that many coaches use to help their clients understand where they are in their lives at any given moment and determine where they want to go. It helped me get clear about what I saw possible for me in my life and get clear about my goals. If you are serious about gaining clarity and crafting a vision, the Wheel of Life exercise will help you. It will not only help you begin to craft your vision, but it will also help you gain clarity on what success looks like in all areas of your life. You will look at where you are right now and your levels of success and happiness in the important areas of your life. It will also get you focused on what

FIRST KEY: DEVELOP A VISION

your ideal level of success and happiness in those areas and you can begin to craft your big goals to make it a reality.

I'm giving you a copy of the Wheel of Life exercise that I developed for my coaching clients. It's helped many of them gain clarity and determine which big goals they should be working on. It will help you do the same. You will gain clarity on what you want in all areas of your life and determine which goals you should be working on right now. You will also begin to develop your vision for your life.

HERE IS HOW TO USE THE WHEEL OF LIFE:

The Wheel of Life is a circle divided into 8 equal parts that represent all of the important areas of your life: your health, family, money, etc. The center, 0 is the least important. The outer line, 10, is the most important. Rate your level of happiness and success in each area on the Wheel. This will give you a visual of where you are in your life right now. If you were to roll the wheel, how smooth or bumpy would it be? In a different color pen or marker, repeat the exercise, and note the ideal number for each area. See the comparison. This will give you an idea of which area you should focus on right now.

The Wheel of Life is a great place to begin to look at where you are and where you want to go in life. It will help you to develop your life vision and your big goals to take action on right now. Take some time to complete the exercise and be honest with yourself.

You can download this worksheet from:
www.YouHaveTheKeysNowDrive.com/resources

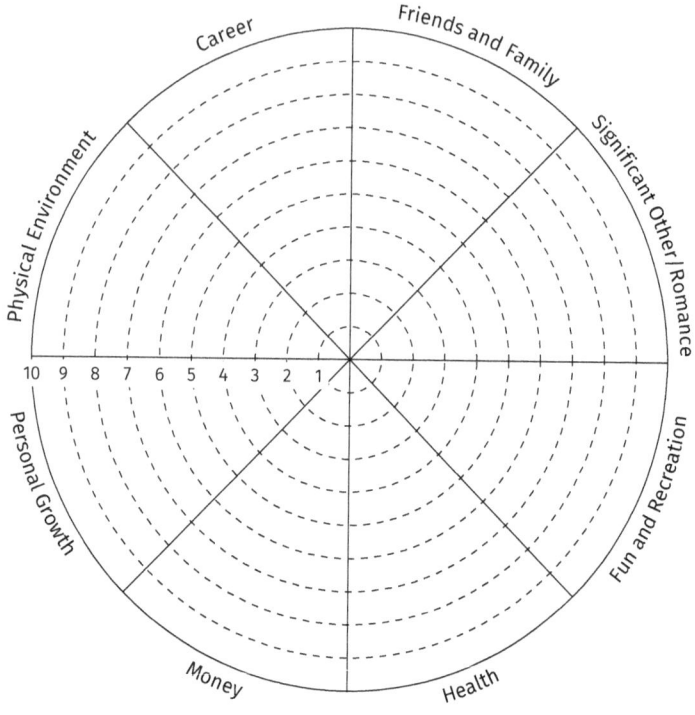

Figure 1.1: *The Wheel of Life*

EXERCISE #2: YOUR LIFE VISION

Journaling can be a powerful exercise to help gain clarity. It is often used in therapy or coaching, or just for people who want to put their thoughts down on paper. It can also help you see your vision in a way that you may have never envisioned it. In this exercise, you will answer powerful questions about yourself and your life to help you craft your life vision. Take time to think about your answers and be honest with yourself. Remember, the more honest you are with yourself, the clearer you will be about what you want and what the best version of yourself looks like. Your vision is an evolving work and you will continue to tweak it over the course of your journey, however, answering the questions below will get you started on crafting your life vision.

FIRST KEY: DEVELOP A VISION

AS YOU ARE ANSWERING THESE QUESTIONS, THINK ABOUT THE FOLLOWING AREAS OF YOUR LIFE:

- Health — exercise, diet, mindfulness, perspective
- Romance – your ideal romantic, loving relationship, your partnership with a significant other
- Family – types of relationships with spouse or partner, children, siblings, parents
- Friends – people you want to surround yourself with, depth of those relationships
- Spirituality – your connection to a higher power, deeper connection with yourself and the universe
- Wealth – finances necessary to make your dreams come true, income to live the life you want
- Career / Business – how will your career or business embody your vision
- Personal Growth – your commitment to learning and growing every day
- Accomplishments – your accomplishments so far and your desire to achieve bigger goals
- Happiness – your happiness and contentment in your life

SOME JOURNALING TIPS FOR YOU:

- Just put pen to paper and write and see what happens!
- Don't worry about grammar or spelling—it's about capturing the essence of your vision
- Quiet the inner critic and let your imagination go

ON A BLANK SHEET OF PAPER WRITE DOWN THESE QUESTIONS AND ANSWER EACH ONE TO THE BEST OF YOUR ABILITY:

1. When I die, what do I want people to remember and say about me?

2. At the end of my life, my greatest accomplishment will be...
3. What is my mission in life that absolutely inspires me?
4. What is my burning passion, what am I truly passionate about?
5. How will my work, career or business enable me to live those dreams?
6. What does my ideal or perfect day look like?
7. If I knew failure wasn't an option, what would I attempt to achieve or do with my life?
8. What do you I want my romantic relationships to be like?
9. What are my secret passions and dreams?
10. In my ideal life, what kind of people are in my life? How do you feel about them?
11. What does my physical body look like? How do I feel about that?

These are questions that most people have never asked themselves. I know I didn't. And because I didn't, I was lost in life. I was making decisions about my career, relationship, finances, even where I wanted to live, based on how I felt at the time. I never had a bigger vision for my life. But doing an exercise like this helped me focus on what's important and keep my vision top of mind when I am out in the world.

One more step for you. Looking at all your answers, try to make one statement about your life vision. Again, think about what you want in all areas of your life, consider the ideal state without any limitations.

HERE ARE A FEW EXAMPLES OF A LIFE VISION STATEMENT:

Here's a short one... Oprah Winfrey's Vision Statement

> *"To be a teacher. And to be known for inspiring my students to be more than they thought they could be."*

Here's a longer one... Another Random Example

> "My life vision is to serve others doing what I love, teaching, coaching and mentoring. I will have the flexibility to do what I want, when I want, with whom I want without worrying about any restrictions. I will have a loving family and a wife who is my partner in all that I do, someone who supports and challenges me to step into my greatness and I do the same with her. My body, mind, and spirit will be the healthiest it's ever been. Spending time with amazing friends who are goal-getters and contributors to the world is what I look forward to. I will be financially wealthy and spiritually connected to my creator and I will continue to be a student of life."

Remember your life vision will be ever-changing and evolving as you grow and develop personally and professionally. It may start off being lengthy like this and then you can shorten it like the previous vision statement. Regardless, it's important for you to know what you truly want in your life. You have to define success and happiness for yourself.

WHEN DO YOU USE YOUR LIFE VISION STATEMENT?

- When you feel lost, stuck, confused or overwhelmed in your life, pause and review your vision
- Before you begin each week, possibly on a Sunday. Take time to read and connect with your vision before starting your week.
- When you are questioning yourself or your purpose or searching for meaning in your life. Re-read your vision and remind yourself that you have a greater mission, a higher purpose in your life.

You can get these downloadable worksheets at www.YouHaveTheKeysNowDrive.com/resources

> **TRY THIS**
>
> 1. Download and complete the **Wheel of Life** exercise
>
> 2. Download and complete **Your Life Vision** exercise, remember to be honest with yourself
>
> 3. Revisit your Wheel of Life and Your Life Vision every 6 to 12 months and adjust and change as you need to
>
> 4. Sign up to the **Driver of Your Destiny** community on Facebook

CHAPTER 2

SECOND KEY: GET TO KNOW YOU

"Know thyself means this, that you get acquainted with what you know, and what you can do."
                                                            —Menander

ARE YOU ready to change your life and live the life that you deserve? Think about it carefully, because I am very serious. Are you really ready to put in the hard work to be who you want to become and live life on your own terms? I am asking you because many people say that they are ready for change and either they are not ready, or they don't know where to begin. Others are not fully committed to putting in the effort that it takes. They know they need to make changes yet cannot make the commitments necessary to succeed.

If you are ready, the next step is to know who you really are. You have to know who you are before you know where you are going. The key to finding your way in life and truly living your dreams is having self-awareness. If you do not know yourself, who you are, and what makes you unique and different from others, you cannot live authentically. You cannot "keep it real" with yourself and those around you.

I have a saying,

"Pretenders can only pretend for so long until their true self is revealed"

You can spend your life living for other people, being unauthentic, but at some point, it will break you down and it will not be a positive experience. In your soul, you will realize that you are not being true to yourself and who you desire to be. You must have a deep understanding of your true, unfiltered, unpolished, honest, authentic self. You need to tap into your greatness and your gifts. It is absolutely necessary for you to reach your end destination of living a happier life.

At some point in life, you may have felt lost. Possibly, you are feeling like something is missing as you are reading these pages, yet you may not be able to pinpoint what it is. You may think that you should be happier because you have a "good job," are in a "good relationship," or you have the body you desire. Or maybe you are earning the salary you always desired, yet for some reason, something is missing. You are not as happy as you want to be. Can you relate to this? I know I could. I have felt this way before and could not understand why. I knew I had many positive things happening in my life, yet something was missing and I just could not figure it out. It wasn't until I remembered the words my grandmother used to say to me growing up that snapped me out of my funk and I figured out why I was feeling a bit lost.

My grandmother used to say that,

"No matter what happens in life, never forget who you are and where you come from"

She used to say that, in life, it is easy to forget your roots, but knowing who you are is like your compass guiding you to your "north star," your center of being. For some people, it is a connection with God. Others get there through meditation, spending time with themselves, or connecting with family and friends. Though you may answer the question "Who are you?" quite frequently in life, do you ever stop to really think about it? You introduce yourself daily and you are often asked whom you are. You most likely state your name and job title if it is a work or networking environment. However, have you truly thought about whom you really are on a deeper level? It is interesting how we often define ourselves and who we are by our job titles and our work. We are so used to talking about work that it dominates many of our conversations even outside of work. We are defined by our job titles. At least, that is what we allow ourselves to believe.

Have you ever been terminated from a job? I know it may be difficult to think about, but you were probably devastated at the time even if you wished for it to happen. What was it about losing the job that was most painful, aside from the obvious financial loss and work relationships? For many of us, losing our jobs is like losing our identity.

We are closely linked with our job titles and we spend one-third of our day at work, so losing your job can be difficult to deal with. The question to ask yourself is, would this loss be less difficult to deal with if you were more confident in who you are as a person? Would knowing the skills and the abilities that you have to offer, not just in terms of being an employee, but also the way you bring yourself into a role, help you through this?

Knowing yourself gives you the confidence you need to go out into the world confident that you will be successful. You will achieve your goals and you develop habits of success. No one can take who you are away from you; it is ingrained in you. People might be able to take material things away from you like a job, a car, or a home, but they cannot take away your life experiences, your values, or your sense of self. That is what will be a tremendous attribute to help you get out of the unstuck.

I AM STATEMENT

Asking yourself powerful questions can help you unlock meaningful answers that you may have been searching for or did not even know you have been searching for. One powerful question to start with is, "*Who am I really?*"

Think of all the qualities that you possess, the ones that make you unique, the ones that your friends, family, and children love about you. Better yet, think about who you were before you got the job, had children, or got into your relationship.

Sometimes we get so swallowed up by life that we don't enjoy living. We don't take time for ourselves and to connect with who we are because we are occupied with a multitude of things. We are too busy being parents, employees, partners, and everything in between to everyone, that we do not pause to connect with ourselves. It is important to be still, to be free from all thoughts and establish a relationship with yourself. The journey begins here. To move towards your best self and your best life, you need to have self-love and self-awareness. You need to be open to what the universe sends your way; you need to create space to allow great things to come to you.

EXERCISE #1: I AM STATEMENT

Before you can begin your journey to change your life, attract more happiness, have more success, and develop stronger relationships; you need to understand who you are and the gifts that you bring to the world. Too often in life people are trying to be someone they are not, or they are too busy taking care of their family and dealing with life. They forget about themselves and lose their true identity. Maybe you can relate.

It is time to get back to who you are. Separate yourself from the job, your partner, your relationships with others, from being a parent/guardian, and focus on yourself. In order to realize how great you truly are you will have an opportunity to answer the series of powerful questions that follow. Take your time and think about your answers. You do not need to rush. This is about connecting with yourself. It is important to answer these questions honestly., Be as open as possible. Do not think about what others would say about your answers. This is about your thoughts, feelings, and emotions. The better you understand your true, authentic self, and the gifts you bring to the world, the more your family, friends, colleagues, and others who interact with you benefit.

Your I Am Statement is your personal affirmation. It is your powerful statement that you can use to overcome stress, to build confidence, and to positively impact your subconscious mind. You may find yourself saying your I Am statement unknowingly because it will be rooted in your mind.

MY ATTRIBUTES

Without over-thinking, in the spaces below, write down 20 attributes to describe yourself. It may seem like a lot, but when you complete the activity you will have a list of awesome words to describe yourself. (i.e. funny, curious, outgoing, etc.). If you cannot think of 20 write down as many as you can. If you are struggling to find words, think of how others describe you.

SECOND KEY: GET TO KNOW YOU

1.	11.
2.	12.
3.	13.
4.	14.
5.	15.
6.	16.
7.	17.
8.	18.
9.	19.
10.	20.

MY FIVE POWERFUL, POSITIVE WORDS

In order to begin to shift your mindset and to walk in your personal power, you have to change your language. You have to change the way you talk to and about yourself. Think of 5 positive, powerful words to describe yourself. Or, think of 5 positive, powerful, words that you would use to describe your future amazing self.

The top 5 positive powerful words or phrases I would use to describe myself are...

1.
2.
3.
4.
5.

There are additional activities within the I Am Statement Worksheet. You will ask yourself powerful questions that will help you tune into who you really are and the amazing qualities that make you unique.

The I Am Statement worksheet is a great tool that asks you powerful questions to help you reconnect with who you are and the gifts that you have to offer the world. It is a self-reflection guide that gets you to focus on things that you love, life challenges that you have encountered, your achievements, and your unique gifts. Take your time and answer all of the powerful questions to craft your "I Am Statement". From there, you will begin to really understand who you are and what you want to achieve most.

When you are stuck, self-reflection and self-exploration will help you to re-establish self-confidence. Having a sense of who you are will help you to regain confidence in your ability to get out of the mud. When you are confident, have higher self-awareness, and know who you truly are (your authentic self), and you can begin pulling yourself free in order to take action.

How often do you take time to reflect on your uniqueness and your sense of being? I would venture to say not very often, if at all. You are probably too busy focusing on your life. You spend so much time focusing on your family, your job, your relationships, and trying to figure out what you want, that you don't take time to reconnect with yourself. In my opinion, having a sense of self, your values, and what is important to you is the basis for making all-important life decisions and committing to changing your circumstances.

Think about all of the decisions that you make in life. How many of those decisions would be different if you made the connection to your authentic self, your life vision and your values? Layer that with understanding your life's purpose and it is quite possible that many of those decisions would be very different. When you live as your authentic self, you are being true to you and your vision of your life, not anyone else's. Understanding the unique gifts that you have to offer the world is something that you can call upon when you are stuck or when you need to make major life decisions later on. Continue to deepen your self-awareness. Take time to self-reflect and meditate, (I will talk about this later in another chapter). You will experience a difference in your ability to get unstuck and your ability to motivate yourself to take action. Having people who will cheer you on or a support network is very important. However, at the end of the day, it is your life and you have to decide how to live it. You are first accountable to yourself for making the changes that you choose to make. Sometimes, you have to call on your inner strength or wisdom to help get you through difficult situations. You can only do that when you have a deep understanding of who you are.

> **TRY THIS**
>
> Go to:
>
> > www.YouHavetheKeysnowDrive.com/resources
>
> to download The **I Am Statement** worksheets and complete them
>
> Revisit your **I Am Statement** every 6 to 12 months and adjust and change as you need to
>
> Sign up to the **Driver of Your Destiny** community on Facebook

You can get these downloadable worksheets at
www.YouHaveTheKeysNowDrive.com/resources

CHAPTER 3

THIRD KEY: PERMISSION TO FAIL

"It's fine to celebrate success, but it is more important to heed the lessons of failure."
    –Bill Gates

GIVE YOURSELF PERMISSION TO FAIL

IN ORDER to achieve great success, you have to step outside of your comfort zone; you have to push and challenge yourself to do more, to do something different. Think of your life; it is full of routines and mundane tasks that you do every day without thinking. Sometimes, you are on autopilot when you don't even realize it. Think about this: how many times do you get to work with no recollection of the drive? Better yet, once you're at work, do you really remember the process of getting up, eating breakfast, getting ready, getting the kids ready, taking them to school and then driving to work? Probably not, because you've done it so many times you simply do everything that needs to be done without even thinking about it. You've gotten too comfortable. Being uncomfortable can help you tap into skills that you did not know you had or allow you to play to your current strengths even more.

In society, we are taught to win; we are taught that winning is the most important thing in life. Rarely does anyone talk about the benefits of losing and what we learn from it. You may have heard coaches talk about winning or watched movies about just that. Usually, the coach is talking about the importance of winning at all costs or how failure is not an option.

Interestingly enough, we relate to that in life. We are afraid to fail and with good reason. In school, we are taught to strive for the highest marks and that failing is not a factor in the equation. Have you ever heard parents say, "Good job on failing that course, what did you learn?" I know I haven't. We all know that in life, there are "winners" and "losers" and the winners seem to have way more fun. They are even idolized and immortalized in some cases. So, who wants to be a loser? No one. However, when we fail, we develop strength, learn to deal with obstacles, and build resilience. Failure teaches us to appreciate success. If we did not fail, we would not fully appreciate our success. What we don't learn is that winners are people who failed and never quit. They are people who learned from their past, developed fierce determination, and keep going on their goals and dreams.

I love this quote by Michael Jordan, considered the greatest professional basketball player of all time.

> "I've missed more than 9000 shots in my career. I've lost almost 300 games. 26 times, I've been trusted to take the game-winning shot and missed. I've failed over and over and over again in my life. And that is why I succeed." –Michael Jordan

Wow! What powerful words from someone who is considered one of the greatest athletes and business people of all time. There are stories of Jordan missing the winning shot in games and staying hours after the game is over to shoot thousands of shots. He didn't quit. He realized that every shot that he missed in a basketball game was painful. However, he used these as and preparation for the game-winning shots he made. You have to look at your life in the same way. For all of your unachieved goals, struggles, challenges, and missteps, you have had wins and success and it's because of the lessons you learned. Failure is a part of the process to becoming successful. Without failure, you can never truly appreciate success.

Give yourself permission to fail and permission to be uncomfortable. I am not saying you should set out to fail, I am saying you should set out to succeed and if you don't get it right the first time you readjust and keep going. It's the fear of failure that holds most people back from even getting started on their goals. How often do you look in the mirror and tell yourself, "Fear will not control my life." Never, right? Fear holds us back from trying new things. It can paralyze our lives and the decisions that we make. Some of those decisions could be life-changing, but we never know because we are living in fear; stuck in the fear of failing. It causes us to stay comfortable, to not challenge or push ourselves towards our greatness. Oh yes, you have greatness within you, you have tremendous gifts for the world. Unfortunately, you are not stepping into it because fear controls that aspect of your life. Do not let it. Do not think about failing; think about succeeding. Failure is merely a roadblock on your journey to living your dreams. It is a pause in your plan, not the end of the road.

Here are some powerful questions for you:

Some of these questions you may have answered in your vision exercise, however, it is always good to revisit it. "What would your life be like if you were not afraid to fail?" Take some time and think about that. If you could not fail, what would you do? What would you attempt to achieve? What impact would that have on your life? Okay, so I asked four powerful questions; however, they are all crafted to help you think about one thing: celebrating fear when you encounter it.

You have choices in life. You make choices every day. You can choose to not let fear run your life. Do not be afraid to fail. If you do experience failure, it is merely a lesson being handed to you on your journey to success.

Most choices you make will not have a major impact on your life; they usually revolve around what you are going to eat, what time you are going to take a coffee break, or what outfit you will wear to work. Making those decisions are routine; however, consider the fact that sometimes you have to make conscious choices to step outside of your comfort zone and stretch yourself. You have to put fear aside and explore new opportunities and possibilities.

Think about failing as a celebration of attempting to do more and be more in life. Stepping outside of your comfort zone is difficult for most people and the fact that it was attempted should be celebrated and used as a lesson learned. The greatest entrepreneurs and CEOs in the world have all failed at some point in their lives. Even Steve Jobs got fired from Apple before later returning as the CEO. We have to shift our thinking about failure in order to get out of flying on autopilot and take control of the plane. You have copilots so that if you fail, they are there to support you and help you get back on track. When you have a support system and believe in yourself, failure is not something to be feared. If it occurs, you will rise again and keep going, because you know you can achieve more and you have support to help you bounce back and keep moving.

Growing up in low-income government housing I never thought I would leave my neighborhood and I most definitely didn't think I would ever move to another province (another state, for my American friends). I was afraid of what was out there in the world. My fear was that I would be out of place and not be accepted, however, I overcame that and stepped outside of my neighborhood. I eventually landed a decent job and I became comfortable in that job and in my life. I showed up every day, however, I wasn't challenged, and I was comfortable and safe being on autopilot. Fear of the unknown paralyzed me. I didn't want to fail, I didn't want to dream big, and I didn't want step outside of my comfort zone. I felt that something was missing and for the longest time, I was afraid to find out what it was. I finally got to the point where I needed to find out what it was.

I decided I needed a change and I left my city, moving 1850 kilometers (1150 miles) away to the big city of Toronto, Canada, with no job, leaving my friends and family behind. I refused to let the fear of failure hold me back from living my true potential. I ended up struggling to find a job; the place I was living did not work out, and I had other failures along the way. Yet, I used those experiences as motivation to continue my journey. I took those failures and celebrated them because out of those failures I learned so much about myself. I had the ability to be resilient and achieve things I didn't know were possible. In the end, it worked out. I found a job that challenged me, a great apartment in the heart of downtown Toronto, and I survived. That's right, I lived through it and I am stronger for it. I am sharing this story because I still have fears and I still wrestle with being uncomfortable. Yet, I know that in order to grow, I cannot let the unknown stop me from living with passion and purpose.

Do not let the idea of failure hold you back; don't let it keep you stuck. You deserve to move forward and achieve greatness in your life.

Do not give failing more attention than you give to what you learn from it, or better yet, don't give it more attention than your *successes*. It is time to give yourself permission to fail, celebrate the idea of failure, and use failure as a lesson. Do not look forward to it; look forward to your success. However, if you do fail, know that you will be fine. You have failed before and overcome those failures, just like you have experienced many successes in your life. Who knows what it will open up for you - a new opportunity, increased resilience, or even lessons for the future. It is your choice. Shift your perspective, dare to dream, and dare to pursue your dreams. Make a choice to continue your pursuit of living a happier life.

DEVELOP THE DISCIPLINE TO FOLLOW YOUR CURIOSITY

By giving yourself permission to fail you are giving yourself permission to explore your curiosity. This is major. Many of the most amazing experiences we have in our lives are not planned. They most likely happen organically or because we do something different. Even when we do plan something, and it turns out to be an amazing experience it usually doesn't happen exactly the way we thought it would. Understanding that failure is a part of growing allows you to get back to your younger self and become curious again. You get back to your big, limitless dreams and you begin to take risks in your life. Successful people are risks takers, they understand that failure is a possibility, but they also understand that the rewards and the lessons learned may be even greater. I'm not just talking about financial rewards; I'm talking about making amazing connections with people who can help you become the best version of yourself. Being curious can lead you to a new career in a field you never thought about. It can lead you to new business opportunities, new life experiences, or a deeper connection to yourself.

Having the discipline to follow your curiosity can lead you to your true gift or talent. It can open up your purpose and lead you to how to share your gift with others. Giving yourself permission to fail, letting yourself know that it is okay to not achieve whatever your goals are to open the door for you to explore new experiences. Real change, life-long change doesn't occur in your comfort zone. It doesn't happen when you do the same things over and over, day after day. That's not where real change happens. Real change and growth happen when you are uncomfortable. It happens when you stretch yourself when you do something you have never done. It happens when you are open to new experiences, places, people and things. I will talk about this more in the next chapter. For now, you must know that fear is a part of moving forward. It is natural to be uneasy with stepping outside of your comfort zone and trying something new. Just remember, if you give yourself permission to fail, you are giving yourself permission to succeed. Failures are lessons and preparation for success. It's time for you to free yourself from past setbacks and challenges and continue on your journey by releasing your emotions from not being where you want to be in your life right now. Trust and believe you are moving towards something greater! In the next chapter, I talk more about following your curiosity and how it will open up opportunities and possibilities in your life.

THIRD KEY: PERMISSION TO FAIL

> **TRY THIS**
>
> 1. On a blank piece of paper, write down something that you failed at. It could be something as small as a test or it could be something like not achieving your weight loss goals. What happened because of the failure? Did you study harder and get an "A" on the next test? Did you start eating healthier or did you become more aware of your body? Think about what you were able to do only because you failed that one time, and then think about something big you're hoping to achieve now and write it down. Look at what you achieved because of failure.
>
> Go to:
>
> www.YouHavetheKeysnowDrive.com/resources
>
> to learn more about goal-setting and how to achieve your goals.
>
> Revisit your **I Am Statement** every 6 to 12 months and adjust and change as you need to.

CHAPTER 4

FOURTH KEY: FOLLOW YOUR CURIOSITY

"We keep moving forward, opening new doors, and doing new things, because we're curious and curiosity keeps leading us down new paths."
—Walt Disney

THERE'S SOMETHING magical about seeing the world through the eyes of a five-year-old. They are full of energy, curious, risk-takers, they are explorers. They have big aspirations for their lives and they truly believe that anything is possible. Even in their failures, mistakes, and accidents they dust themselves off, learn from them, get up and keep moving. Kids are really good at being creative and following their curiosity. My question is, what happened to you? Where did your five-year-old self disappear to?

Some people are really great at keeping that curiosity, while others see their goals, dreams, and desires as things that are unattainable. When I see people who have achieved extraordinary things in their lives, I see people who have had the discipline to follow their curiosity.

To me, this ability to remain curious is just as, if not more important, than having a plan. We are all curious about many things, however, most of us do not act on our curiosity. Instead we continue to think about whatever it is we are curious about and it fades into the background and re-surfaces from time to time. If you want a shift, a huge transformation in who you are and in living the life you want, you must have the discipline to follow your curiosity.

It is all about taking action. Your small daily actions, lead to bigger wins, which lead to a huge shift in your life and within you. The problem with most people and their curiosity is that they think they need an elaborate plan before they can do ANYTHING and because of that, they do NOTHING. Does this sound familiar? I know I can relate. I used to be just like that. I was curious about many things and I thought I needed elaborate goals plans to even take the first step to explore my curiosity. Because of that, I was overwhelmed and did nothing. It wasn't until I realized that I did not need a plan I just needed to act on my curiosity that my life began to shift in a big way. I moved from a small city to the biggest city Toronto. I began to travel the world and go to places I used to dream about, Brazil, Thailand, Jamaica, Spain and more. My confidence increased and I began to attract career opportunities that I thought were out of my league. I became an author, business owner, and speaker. Things began to happen.

When you decide that you have this burning desire to learn more, do more, explore more about something that has been on your mind for a long time, something changes. When you commit to doing something about it, your life changes. It's just like that! You can form a plan along the way, but the key to finishing strong is getting started.

What are you curious about? A new job or starting your own business? Do you want to learn more about how you can make more money? Is there a place that you have always wanted to travel to but haven't been yet? Are you curious about how to lose weight or meet your fitness goals? Do you want to buy a home? Are you searching for a life partner, someone who will build you up and bring out the best in you? Are you thinking about going to school or taking a course? If you are feeling stuck in your life or have something stirring in the back of your mind ask yourself two questions. The first question is, **What am I curious about right now**? The second question is, **what am I going to do about it**?

Having the discipline to follow your curiosity and make decisions will lead you to where you are meant to be in your life. Have you ever wondered why some people are so happy all the time? They are always smiling, cheerful, and laughing, and you just don't get it. You probably can't stop glancing at them over your shoulder and staring at them. Does it annoy you that they are enjoying themselves? Well, they are fully experiencing and enjoying life. They are absolutely happy no matter what is going on around them and no matter what anyone says to them. Do you find that annoying? You should, because they appear

FOURTH KEY: FOLLOW YOUR CURIOSITY

to be living their life's purpose and you are not. They are enjoying the little things in life and have an appreciation for what they have. You should be jealous. After all, I know I am a little jealous and I *am* doing what I love.

I once met a waitress who was so cheerful and so full of energy that she could not stop smiling. She was bubbly and happy and I found it very annoying. I asked her what she was "on," jokingly assuming anyone that happy had to be taking some kind of "happy pills." She replied, "Nothing, I love my job." I said to her, "You love being a waitress? Aren't some people rude to you, or difficult to serve?" She responded, "Yes, some people are difficult, but most people are friendly, and the ones who are difficult maybe just having a bad day, or have some other bad things happening in their life right now. I try to make their day a little better."

I was amazed at her answer; she was trying to inject happiness into people's lives by serving them with a smile and being friendly and cheerful. Wow! What a concept: to love your job and to actually make other people's day more enjoyable. Do people actually do that? The answer is: Yes!

"I love what I do." Do you love what you do? I am passionate about coaching people, training them, and helping them on their journey to reach their potential. But until I met that waitress, I never realized how "loving what you do" could have such an impact. After speaking with her, I thought maybe I come across like that when I'm doing what I love. Maybe, my energy shines through when I see someone have an "Ah-ha" moment because they just shifted their perspective and were able to see a situation in a different light.

I hope I don't come across as too over-the-top when I am doing what I love, but when I am happy and feeling great about what is happening in my life, other people feel it. Other people can see your values and passion as well. They see how you light up when you are doing what you love, and it does not have to be a job. It can be raising your children, volunteering, hosting family gatherings, doing a hobby, or anything that gives you energy. When you are living your values, passion, and purpose, life is not only enjoyable, but it has meaning. A chain reaction begins because your life has meaning, the important decisions that you make are more meaningful. Think about what your life will be like when you have a sense of meaning when you are passionate about doing what you love. I am sure it will be much more rewarding. When you make decisions and challenge yourself from a positive perspective, you will be able to achieve "unbelievable" accomplishments.

> "When your values are clear to you, making decisions becomes easier."
>
> –Roy E. Disney

REMEMBER YOUR VALUES

Your values are important because they act as anchors for how you live your life. They guide how you make decisions, how you treat others, how you raise your children and many other important aspects of your life. We all have values; however, not all of us are true to those values. For example, a person may think it's wrong to lie, but they work for a company that lies about their profits by exaggerating numbers a little for board meetings. That's definitely not in line with their values, but they still work for the company because they are comfortable, they know the job, or they may have a fear of seeking employment elsewhere. This is common for many of us, not that we are exaggerating numbers, however, we do things that are disconnected from our values and who we are. It may be working for a company that is completely unaligned with your values and beliefs, not spending as much time as you want to with your family, or having a negative self-image and treating yourself poorly. Regardless of how you are not being true to your values, it is essential to re-connect with your guiding principles and beliefs in order to move forward and achieve your goals.

There may be many reasons why you are not living your values. One reason is that you may be disconnected from them. You may have encountered many difficulties in life or many toxic people along the way and it has swayed you from your what is important in your life. You may be so busy with living life, taking care of your family and working, that you don't spend much time thinking about what you need to be happy. Maybe a major life experience occurred; you have lost faith and have thrown away your values. No matter what situation you are in your values are a part of who you are – they are always with you. Your experiences, relationships, and environment shape how you see the world and how you behave in it. Life is not always easy and sometimes in the midst of the uneasiness, challenges, and interaction with saboteurs, you lose yourself. Now is the time to find yourself; to make a deep connection to your beliefs, values, and spirituality. It is your choice: either stay connected, reconnect with those values, or ignore them and pack them away. However, even if you have locked them away, they never leave you; they are always present. You cannot throw away who you are; it is ingrained in your spirit. Your values are your deep understanding of what you believe to be true and what is important to you.

Taking time to reflect on who you are and the gifts that you have to offer to the world helps you to shift perspective. When you are able to start shifting your perspective you can get unstuck and see the light at the end of the tunnel. Yes, that's all it's going to take. I know, easier said than done. If you devote time to reflect and see your life situations from different perspectives, you can change your entire life. Take some time to reflect on your values to find out what they are. What will living with your values do for you in life? What is the impact on others when you live your values? These are powerful questions to ask yourself to help you get out of your rut and to make important changes in your life.

PASSION AND PURPOSE

We often use 'passion' and 'purpose' interchangeably and consider finding our passions in life the same as finding our life's purpose. I disagree. I believe they are different and that it is important to make the distinction between them when trying to determine how they factor into your life.

Let me start by defining "passion" and "purpose." According to the Merriam-Webster dictionary, "passion" is defined as a strong feeling of enthusiasm or excitement for something or about something. This is why sometimes people refer to a romance as "passionate." They have a strong feeling for what they share with another person. You may also consider sports fans as being extremely passionate about their sports teams or sports figures.

"Purpose" is defined as the reason why something is done or used; the aim or intention of something. The aim or goal of a person: what a person is trying to do, become, etc. An example would be you going to school for twelve years. Your purpose is to reach graduation day.

Do you see the difference? When you are passionate about something, it gives you energy, it's fun, and you love to do it. When you have a purpose, it is a *reason* for doing what you're doing; it is what a person is trying to achieve or become. The two can be the same; however, they are not *always* the same.

For example, I am passionate about music, food, traveling, sports, and many other things, yet it doesn't mean any of those are my life's purpose. In fact, my life purpose in life is to help other people live with passion and purpose. I love to help people be their authentic selves and follow their dreams.

The reason I make a distinction between the two is that if you truly want to live purposefully, then you need to understand what it means. A life's purpose is what you are meant to do, it's about what your legacy will be at the time you depart the Earth. It can be anything; after all, it is personal to you. No one can tell you what your life's purpose is, they can only help you articulate it and formulate what it looks like to you. For some people, it can be to help the less fortunate rise out of poverty, for others it may be to raise their children to be productive, respectful adults who follow their dreams. Another person may want to be an entertainer and create a memorable body of work; for someone else, it could be sharing his or her talents with others. It's different for everyone.

Another important message is that your life purpose is not determined or defined by anyone else. It is your understanding of your calling. It is what you want to give and leave the world - your legacy. It means if you want to be an entertainer, it is not "silly" and it's no

FOURTH KEY: FOLLOW YOUR CURIOSITY

less important than your spouse wanting to become CEO of his or her company. Both of you have the right to have a life purpose and for that purpose to be whatever you want most to achieve.

The challenge for some people is discovering their purpose and believing it is possible to live it out loud. In some cases, it is hard work. It may not come easily to you; you may have to dig deep and really think about it. In doing the work, you will discover your purpose; and it's usually right in front of you. It is just blocked by everything you have going on in life.

You are so busy working, raising families, paying bills, trying to get out of debt, maintaining relationships, running this way and that, you don't have time to think about what you really want out of life or what your legacy will be. That's understandable. However, you deserve more; you deserve to be happy, to be successful, to be free to spend more time with loved ones, and it is time to tell yourself just that.

Maybe you are not at the point in life where you want to put in the work to discover or live your purpose. You might not want to put forth the effort, time, and dedication to living your purpose. It's fine; I get it. However, ask yourself, "What will I gain from living my life's purpose?" "How will living my life's purpose enrich my life and the lives of those around me?" If you answer those questions and you are still fine with not pursuing the life you were meant to live, then you should be happy with continuing on your current life path. You can always pursue your purpose in the future. It is never too late to discover what you are truly meant to do.

Finding purpose in life is finding meaning, discovering what you are passionate about, and then living up to what you feel you are meant/destined to do on this earth. A few questions to ask yourself: "How can I use my special skills or talents to serve the world?" "What can I do to help others?" "If I was able to make a speech on live television and it was watched by hundreds of millions of people across the world, what message would I deliver?" Answering these questions will help you to begin to identify your purpose in life. The next step, of course, is to take action.

Think of what you can do to live your purpose. It could be spending more time with your loved ones, volunteering, sharing your talents with others, or any other action that you can identify for yourself. Some people never uncover their life's purpose; others know it, but do not live it because they think it is not possible. Shake off those negative vibes because it is absolutely possible to live your life's purpose. Lots of people are doing it and you can too. Are you living your life's purpose? What is your life's purpose? To what extent are you living your life's purpose? If you are not, why not? Is it because a voice in your head is telling you that you cannot do it? Or, even worse, does that voice ask, "What will happen if I achieve my goal and live my life's purpose?" Those mind tricks shackle us and keep us still, stuck, and a slave to fear. This is tough talk, but it is true! That is why it is important to silence the negative voice. Don't let anyone get in the way of your dreams...including yourself.

SILENCE THE VOICES AND CRITICS

Chasing your dreams is something that some of you think about and others take action on. Somewhere along the way, while you're rising out of the mud, you get derailed and it is usually because a "voice" started talking to you. You know which voice I am talking about. It typically says things like, "You can't do that," or, "You are not smart enough to do that," or, "Your mom/dad/spouse would never let you do that so don't even try it." Some may call "the voice" a saboteur; however, it may not resonate with you because, in most situations, the voice is someone you know on a personal level and maybe close to you. It could be someone you interact with on a daily basis, like your spouse, a friend, or family member. It could be someone you haven't talked to for a long time, like a grade school teacher. The person doesn't really need to be face-to-face with you in order for their voice to bring you down. It could also be a memory or a thought of some not-so-pleasant interaction in the past that continues to live within you. The voice will be loud and clear when you declare what you want in life and start moving toward it.

If the people close to you are consistently not happy for you when you achieve your goals, they are saboteurs. It could also be a situation

FOURTH KEY: FOLLOW YOUR CURIOSITY

that happened in the past that had a negative effect on you that has stuck with you when you attempted to move forward. A saboteur is someone or something that tries to stop your progress. The closer you get to achieving what you want in life, the louder the voices become. They are holding you back and keeping you in the mud. Saboteurs are very sneaky, they appear to have your best interest at heart, often rationalizing reasons why you shouldn't live your dreams or achieve your goals.

I'm not talking about hearing your spouse's voice in your head when you are going to buy that extra pair of shoes or the latest gadget that you probably do not need. That's not "the voice" or the saboteur; that is probably a rational person looking out for your best interests. Your spouse knows that you shouldn't spend money haphazardly and they are trying to help with that goal. What I am talking about is when you attempt to achieve a goal in life and the saboteur intrudes and "rationalizes" why you cannot achieve your goal. That voice even makes it sound logical to the point where you give up on your goal and continue doing what you have always done simply because you believe they know better than you. It's the definition of insanity.

Les Brown, one of the leading motivational speakers in the world, is quoted as saying, "Someone's opinion of you does not have to become your reality." He says that you have greatness within you and no one can take it away from you. He's right, you need to put the negative voices and people aside, or use them as motivation to light a fire to achieve your goals. Do not allow others to stop you from moving forward in life; do not allow yourself to get in your own way. No one else can live your life for you; do not allow them to determine your successes or failures.

You are responsible for your life; no one else. Do not live your life for other people. Remember, I talked about the best friend scenario earlier. You may encounter situations that are similar, relationships that are somewhere in the middle of helping and hurting. Don't let those relationships or anything else stop you from dreaming big and taking action. YOU must determine what YOU want in your life and go and get it. We often settle in our jobs, relationships, and put off our goals because most people around us do the same. We think our coworkers are not happy in their jobs and we settle. Or we see some of our family members or friends in unfulfilling relationships and we stay in ours. Even though we know that we deserve a partner that is much more supportive, loving, and encouraging. Rarely do we come across a person living their life's purpose, and if we do we think they are one of the "lucky ones". We think this is the way life is so we accept it. We think that no one ever gets what they really want in life so we might as well just be happy with what we have. You cannot accept mediocrity. You should never accept it. Always strive for greatness. You deserve more for yourself and for your loved ones. You deserve to live a happier, charged life.

It all begins with taking action, and then you must believe that you deserve to win. You must declare it to the universe and stay focused until you accomplish your goals. It is not easy; you have to be brave. You have to be willing to be uncomfortable because change is uneasy. You even have to expect setbacks and roadblocks. Isn't it worth the hardships to get unstuck, to walk out of the mud, to feel great about your life? Don't you owe it to yourself and your loved ones to take steps towards being fulfilled?

Once you find your life's purpose, you can begin to take steps to live it. The problem is that it takes courage to even utter the words "life's purpose." Most people think only a chosen few will find and live their dreams. We are actually programmed to think this way. In some cases, society, school, and even our jobs make us think we should conform and be happy doing what everyone else is doing. We think that since everyone else is following the rules and falling in line, we should too. Living your dreams sometimes means not following the rules, not conforming, and not wanting to be like everyone else.

Think of Elon Musk, Richard Branson, and Arianna Huffington. They have all been rule-breakers and dared to step outside the norm. Look online at what they have achieved and what they overcame to get where they are today. You will no doubt be amazed and find many other famous and not so famous people who have made similar changes. I'm not saying that you have to take leaps as they did, maybe just start with a few steps. You may already be doing what you love. That's great, keep doing it, and tell people that you are doing it.

You also may not be living the life you want because some things may be holding you back: finances, family responsibilities, or other problems. It happens. The question is, have you really sat down and thought about what you want your legacy to be? How do you want to be remembered and for what? What can you do to make the world a better place?

You see, situations in life are all about perspective. You can choose to look at hardships in many different ways. Sometimes, a negative experience can - develop into an important lesson to be learned. By shifting your perspective and connecting it back to your values, life's purpose and your passions, it helps you focus on situations that are out of focus. It helps you make important life decisions in the context of your bigger picture.

I have developed two tools to help you find your passions and life purpose. These tools are designed to think about your life in ways that you may not have thought about in the past. Taking the time to complete these worksheets will provide more clarity around what you are passionate about in your life and your life's purpose.

EXERCISE #1: FINDING YOUR PASSION AND PURPOSE

This exercise is designed to help you unlock your true passions, to find the things that you really enjoy doing or that you are curious about, and show you how you can do more of what you love. You will also learn the questions that you should be asking yourself to help you find your real purpose, your gift. Right now, we are going to focus on helping you discover your true passions and your real gift, your purpose, the thing you were born to do.

On a blank piece of paper, write down and answer these questions: What are you passionate about? What gives you energy? What are you curious about? These are questions that you probably never ask yourself. As a result, you probably don't know your passions and are not playing to them as much as you could be. In this exercise, you will think about your hobbies, interests, childhood memories, curiosities, and how you can be of service to others to help you find your passions and purpose. The other thing that is important to note is that you may realize that some of the questions you are answering are similar to others from previous exercises. The reason for this is that if you truly want personal change, you have to ask yourself some of the same questions and try to answer them as they relate to different aspects of your life. If you truly want personal change you need to be open to doing things differently and being consistent in developing yourself personally and professionally.

HOBBIES AND INTERESTS

Your interest and hobbies are a good place to begin to search for your passions. They are often indicators of your true passions and activities that you enjoy doing.

Take some time to answer questions about what you enjoy doing in your free time, what you would do if money was not an issue and other questions related to your hobbies and interests. Maybe you enjoy reading to your kids, maybe you like to exercise, or you enjoy volunteering. Whatever your interests and hobbies, they may be leaving you clues to unlock your true passions and purpose. Answer the questions below. Don't overthink your answers. On a blank piece of paper write it down these questions and your answers.

1. What activities do I love doing in my free time?
2. What would I do even if I didn't get paid?
3. What could I do for hours and still be excited about doing?
4. What activities give me energy when I am doing them?
5. If I won the lottery tomorrow how would I spend my time?
6. What activities or interests am I curious about right now?

You can get the downloadable worksheets at www.YouHaveTheKeysNowDrive.com/resources

I knew at a young age that I wanted to help people in some way. It is something that has been and still is a constant in my life. I continue to work at jobs and volunteer in places that allow me to be of service.

My grandmother was a big influence in that regard. She was a generous person and always helping others. When she passed away, I felt a lot of emotions and I was left trying to figure out why she had to leave us. For weeks, I was angry, confused, upset, and I didn't know what to do. I was disconnected from who I was, and I was not concerned with doing anything productive. One day, I just sat down and thought about my grandmother and all of the great memories that we had together. I began to look at her passing in a different way. I thought about the values that she instilled in me, the fun times and our conversations about my desire to help others and my dreams. In reflecting on those conversations, I was able to reconnect with my values, passions, and began my journey to find my life purpose.

It helped me to realize how instrumental she was in establishing the foundation for who I am today, and I took that as a catalyst to continue to live my greatness. The way she lived inspired me to live the way I want to live, and I do that by knowing myself, understanding my values, my passions and my purpose in life. This is not to say I am living her vision of what my life should be; However, she helped me realize I needed to choose my own path and be true to myself. This is what I want for you. I want you to re-connect with your values, passions and find your true mission or purpose in life. It's definitely possible for you, and it starts with the decisions that you make. The more you take risks, follow your curiosity and take action on making important decisions, the closer you will get to becoming the person you are meant to be.

EXERCISE #2: LIFE DECISIONS WORKSHEET

When you are connected to what is important in your life your ability to move forward and make better decisions is amplified. Are you facing a major life decision right now? Is it something you have been struggling with for a while? I have developed a Life Decisions worksheet that will assist you in making a sound decision.

The Life Decisions Worksheet will help you make informed decisions about things that are important to you. Sometimes it is difficult to make major decisions in your life for many reasons. Maybe you are afraid to change; other people in your life may be trying to strongly influence you to decide one way or another, or you may have too many complicated factors to consider. The Life Decision Worksheet will help you map out your thoughts in a logical way, and will help you remove some of the emotion and anxiety around your decision by looking at it from a more objective perspective.

On a blank piece of paper, write down and answer these questions:

1. The big decision that I have to make is...
2. I want or need to make this decision because...
3. If I don't make this decision, will I regret it? Yes or no, explain
4. List all of the advantages of making the decision.
5. List all of the disadvantages of making the decision.
6. Who am I making the decision for? How will it affect others?
7. How will I feel after I make this decision? Is this decision aligned with my values and beliefs? Explain.
8. What would my mentor, coach, or role model do?
9. What does my heart say?
10. My decision is...
11. The reason for my decision is...

You can get the downloadable worksheets at: www.YouHaveTheKeysNowDrive.com/resources

The Worksheet will help you look at the pros and cons, how your decision is connected to your values, passions, and life purpose, and help you decide if you should get other people involved. This Worksheet will help you remove high levels of anxiety and emotion from decisions that often paralyze you and keep you stuck (in the mud?). This is not to say that you should not utilize emotion or be anxious or concerned when making decisions. It is about controlling those feelings to allow you to make rational decisions that could have a significant effect on your life.

Both I and my clients used this Worksheet to make major life decisions. We all agree that it has indeed helped us make more sound decisions in a rational way. We were able to make decisions that we had been struggling with for years in a much shorter time frame by utilizing this Worksheet.

On your road to following your curiosity and finding your passion and purpose, remember to stay true to your values. Don't lose who you are on your quest to find out who you are meant to be. You will struggle along the way, you will be challenged, you will have to make life-changing decisions. That's all part of the journey. Chase your dreams and be open to new experiences and opportunities and you will end up right where you are supposed to be.

> **TRY THIS**
>
> Download and complete the Finding Your **Passion and Purpose** Worksheet
>
> Download and complete the **Life Decisions** Worksheet
>
> Join the **Driver of Your Destiny** community on Facebook

You can get these downloadable worksheets at
www.YouHaveTheKeysNowDrive.com/resources

CHAPTER 5

FIFTH KEY: YOUR LIFE SUPPORT NETWORK

> *"My friends and family are my support system. They tell me what I need to hear, not what I want to hear and they are there for me in the good and bad times. Without them, I have no idea where I would be and I know that their love for me is what's keeping my head above the water."*
> —Kelly Clarkson

QUOTES ARE amazing. They are powerful words that have deep meaning. Often they make us think about our own lives, they inspire us to take action and they can change our perspective. If you are like me, you may have grown up hearing your parents, grandparents, or other adults drilling life lessons into your head.

"Show me your friends and I'll tell you who you are."

That's one of the keys to life that my late grandmother, Mrs. Monica Stone, used to say to me all the time. It is a powerful statement that I now realize has deep meaning and importance in my life. In fact, it changed my life forever. I will tell you how later.

My grandmother passed away in 2004, after losing her fight with cancer at 71 years old. Of course, it was a huge loss for our family. She was the matriarch who helped each one of her children and grandchildren in ways we probably didn't deserve (realize?). Before I get into this key to life, let me tell you a bit about my grandmother, friend, and mentor. She and I had a very special bond. Even though she was my grandmother, we were the best of friends. She was my mentor, we both loved our after work or evening get-togethers. She would give me all types of life lessons; lessons about being confident, achieving goals, career advice. We talked about many things.

We had this understanding and appreciation that we have similarities and differences and that always led to amazing conversations and discoveries for both of us. My grandmother was a small (5'4"), but mighty, Jamaican woman who grew up tough in the countryside in Jamaica. She worked the farm like her brothers and was just like one of the guys. She met my grandfather Lloyd and they married and eventually moved to Canada in the 1960s. Growing up I remember my grandmother as being loving and caring, someone who always had time to help others. If someone was sick she would make soup and take it to them. If they were having financial trouble she would find a way to give them a few extra dollars. And if they were in the hospital she would be there to visit. I also remember her being a stern, tell-it-like it is, straight shooter. If she saw any type of injustice or mistreatment of others she would definitely come to their defense. She would help them understand their situation, but without them feeling as if they'd been scolded or yelled at. they understood without yelling, it was more in an assertive way. She also had this really gentle way of getting you to see the truth about yourself. She could make you dig deep and answer questions about yourself you didn't even know needed answering.

The woman was special. Everyone who met her knew that there was just "something about Mrs. Stone." She was real. She admitted her flaws and worked on them and continued to better herself. She always surrounded herself with positive people, people who were moving forward in life. Of course, she had her flaws like any other person. She could be very stubborn and she could be very outspoken at times, but we all have things to work on. I know I am going on about my grandmother, however, I had to let you know the back-story before I share the key that she gave me. I should also tell you that she is a huge part of me being who I am today.

Back to the quote, I mentioned earlier. One of the major keys that my grandmother passed on to me was...

"Show me your friends and I'll tell you who you are."

It is a powerful life lesson, and as I mentioned earlier, it truly changed my life. What it means is that you are who you associate with. If you spend most of your time with negative people you will become a negative person. If you hang around people with limited goals and dreams, you will have limited goals and dreams. If you are close to people who take action and pursue greatness, you will pursue greatness.

I learned this lesson first hand. Growing up in an inner-city, low-income housing community, I was surrounded by drugs, violence, and crime. Many of the people I associated with were criminals, negative people that tried to get ahead by bringing other people down. I realized that in order for me to grow and achieve bigger goals than becoming the best drug dealer, I needed to change the people I spent time with. I made the decision to not only change the people that I hung around with, but I also changed my environment by going away to university. When I changed my inner circle, my entire world changed. I went to university and came back to work in my community as a youth worker and mentor. My life opened up. My belief in myself and what was possible had me fired up about chasing my dreams. The new group of friends and mentors that I spent my time with were supportive and challenged me to keep moving forward. Life was different because the people I was around were different. They were positive, "goal-getters", and they encouraged me to set bigger goals.

This may be a lesson that you need to get hold of. You need to ask yourself: are the people I spend the most time with, holding me back or helping me move forward in my life? Are my friends, family, co-workers, and mentors encouraging me to live a bigger life? Do they encourage me to become the best version of myself or not? Those are very powerful, life-changing questions.

Most people won't ask themselves these questions out loud because they know the answers. They know that some or most of the people that spend time with are not encouraging. These individuals may be very negative, constantly telling them why they shouldn't try something new or set bigger goals. Maybe you can relate. Maybe there are people in your life who are in your driver's seat telling you why you should live small, why your dreams will never become a reality, why you will never have the financial stability you want in your life.

Maybe your mother, father, sister, brother, son, daughter, cousin, grandmother, grandfather, husband, wife, boyfriend, girlfriend, teacher, manager, coworker, or acquaintance are standing in your way. They may be blocking the door to the driver's seat. They don't want you to take that journey to greatness because they are afraid you will leave them behind. The thing is, it's not their journey. It's yours! Do not let anyone get in your way to becoming the person you want to become and achieving the goals that you want to achieve. You **have** to be the driver.

There is something within you that knows your life has meaning and purpose and it wants to be unleashed. You have gifts within you that need to be shared. You have to put yourself first. You have to surround yourself with people who build you up. People who energize you, charge you up, get you excited about your goals and dreams. You need to spend your time with people who are positive. Choose to be around people who are driven, people who are drivers, people who take action. Time is too precious to be around people who steal your energy. You don't need to be in the company of people who are negative. Spend your time with family, friends, relatives, coworkers, and mentors who will help you to get to your end destination, wherever that is for you in your life.

Here's the interesting thing, when you begin to change your perspective, when you change your mindset and make up your mind that your goals and dreams are worthy of action, people will change. One of two things will happen with those you choose to spend time with you. Either they will elevate their perspective and something ignites a spark within them to dream bigger, love harder, and pursue their passions and purpose; or they will stop talking to you. They stop talking to you and sometimes the jealousy and envy comes your way because you are doing something they are not yet brave enough to do live fully. It is difficult for people who are living in the middle, people who are in unfulfilling relationships, uninspiring, or who lack self-confidence, to be happy for you. You chasing your goals is a reminder to them that they are not! A passenger cannot be happy for a driver when they wish they were behind the wheel but are too afraid to jump into the driver's seat.

FIFTH KEY: YOUR LIFE SUPPORT NETWORK

It's time to ask yourself, "Do I have the life support system I need to help me on my journey to living an extraordinary life?" If you do, then that's awesome. Continue to check in with your support team on a regular basis and call upon them when you are struggling with your goals. If you do not have the support you need you must seek out people who will build you up.

Find mentor, friends, coworkers, and other supportive people who will help you raise the bar in your life. Think about people you know. Who can help you in the areas of your life that you are trying to develop? Maybe you want to increase your fitness; do you know someone who is very active in the gym? Maybe you are trying to get on track with your finances; do you know someone who is great with theirs? Maybe you are struggling in your career; do you know someone who loves their job or who has started their own business? Connect with them. If you don't know anyone who can help you with your goals, there are other options. You can find mentors, teachers, trainers and free communities online to help you.

HERE ARE SOME PLACES YOU CAN USE TO BEGIN TO BUILD YOUR LIFE SUPPORT NETWORK.

- Facebook Groups
- Google Groups
- My free **Driver of Your Destiny** Community
- LinkedIn
- Local Meetups
- Ask Friends to Recommend Coaches, Trainers, Teachers
- Search Life Coaches, Personal Trainers, Financial Planners and Other Professionals online

I have an activity at the end of this chapter that you can do to help you look at your current Life Support System to see if they are the people you need to help you live the life you want. If you need additional people to help you figure it out, motivate you, hold you accountable, or provide you with guidance, this activity will help you.

Changing your life can be uncomfortable. It requires dedication and determination. It is not easy to set and achieve goals or, for that matter, to get unstuck and move forward. That is why you need a support system. You need people to support and motivate you during those moments of frustration, and challenges, or when toxic voices appear to de-motivate you and stop your progress. There are many times that you may feel defeated in your quest to achieve your goals. It is during those times that you need to call upon people who have your best interests at heart, who will encourage you, and hold you accountable.

LIFE SUPPORT NETWORK

Who are the people in your support network? Who are the people who hold you accountable for doing what you say you are going to do? Who are the people who inspire you in times when you are not motivated to follow through on your action plan?

You need people to support your progress; cheerleaders and champions who are in your corner; people who want to see you succeed. These are not people who tell you what you want to hear or allow you to accept defeat. They are people who care about you and support you in achieving what you want in life. There are times in life, some more so than others, where you think you can do it all by yourself. However, dealing with the difficulties of managing relationships, caring for your family, managing the demands of your job, handling your financial responsibilities, and pursuing your goals are challenging. It is a lot to manage alone, yet some of us still think we can do it. Instead, reach out and connect with people who care about you. Having a support system will take you to unimaginable heights.

I call this your Life Support Network. I am not referring to a system that someone is connected to when they are in the hospital. Rather, it is your group of family, friends, coworkers, neighbors, or network group members who will support you in getting unstuck and overcoming barriers. They are people you trust, value, and admire, who keep you motivated, and honest, and who will hold you accountable for doing what you say you will do. When you share your goals with people, you

FIFTH KEY: YOUR LIFE SUPPORT NETWORK

are more likely to be successful because you are not only accountable to yourself, but others as well.

The Life Support Network tool will help you identify people you can reach out to for support during your journey.

Here's an exercise to help you look at your Life Support Network:

1. On a blank piece of paper make 4 columns

2. In the first column write **Name of Person** (list people you are close to that you will tell about your goals; only supportive people)

3. In the second column write **Relationship to Me** (what is their relationship to you? Family member, friend, coach, coworker)

4. In the third column write **Frequency I Will Check-in With Them** (how often will you connect with them to discuss your progress?)

5. In the fourth column write, **How They Will Hold Me Accountable** (will you have a weekly phone call, in-person meeting, Skype call)

You do not have to tell many people about your goals and dreams. It's more important to find just a few people to support and encourage you. You need people to hold you accountable for doing what you say you will do. Again, be VERY careful who you chose to tell about your goals. As I said earlier, not everyone will support you, so limit talking about your goals to those individuals.

You can get the downloadable worksheets at www.YouHaveTheKeysNowDrive.com/resources

Take some time to think about people who will support you in your journey to change your life. Complete the worksheet and reach out to the individuals that you identified as members of your Life Support Network. Make sure you check in with them often to inform them of your progress or when you are struggling. You will be amazed at your ability to accelerate the amount of time it takes to achieve your goals when you have people motivating and supporting you along the way.

GET A COACH

A life coach can help you realize what you want in life in a way that other people in your support network cannot. A coach can work with you to unlock the answers that you hold within yourself and motivate you to take action and steer the course. Another benefit is that your life coach is not your personal friend or family member. That means their only objective is to help you do what's best for you without any private agenda. The most successful people in the world have coaches; from everyday people to athletes, to entrepreneurs, to CEOs, too many other accomplished individuals.

Think of the products that Bill Gates has produced and led to the production of, in his reign as Microsoft CEO. He was able to produce the most widely used computer software in the world, Microsoft Office, which is now used by almost 750 million people. He admits that it was a coach who helped him to excel at Microsoft and take the company to the level of success he was able to achieve prior to leaving. Steve Jobs also stressed the importance of everyone having a coach. He talked about how it helped him revolutionize Apple. Like Gates and Jobs, you need someone who will work with you to ask you powerful questions, someone to help you dig deep and shift perspectives. A life coach can help you do that and work with you to hold your agenda of what is important to you. They will also keep you accountable.

I am not saying this because I'm a success coach and have seen the transformations that my clients have achieved. I am saying this because I have seen the success that I have achieved in my personal and professional life by having a coach of my own. Think about this: you are struggling in some area in your life or you want more happiness or success. You have been trying to do it on your own for years yet have been unsuccessful. You have people who support you, and you may even be motivators yet, you still have not achieved what you want in life. Maybe you make progress then become unmotivated or other things simply get in the way. How can you change that and move forward? You can do it by working with a coach.

A coach will help guide you through the difficulties, exhilaration, and of attempting to change your life. With all of the commitments that you have in life, things can get in your way and hold you back without you even realizing it. Coaches will ask you powerful questions, help you change your perspective and assist you in dealing with the obstacles that you will encounter. They will help you tap into your motivations to develop patterns that will drive your success.

Here are some of the benefits of working with a life coach:

- Help you gain clarity about what you want, why you want it, and how to achieve it.
- Assist in developing a strategy to help you get from where you are now to your end destination.
- Assist with overcoming challenges and roadblocks.
- Shift your perspective to help you budge from where you are stuck.
- Support, motivate and hold you accountable for doing what you say you will do.
- Help you achieve more balance in your life.

When seeking a coach, you should look for someone who has been professionally trained, someone with whom you connect and have a good rapport, and who offers a sample session. Sample sessions are typically free, short 15-30 minute coaching sessions where you have an opportunity to experience being coached. It is also an opportunity to evaluate the coach and determine if you resonate with their coaching style. During the session, you will discuss what you are looking to get out of the coaching engagement. You will learn more about the coach and their coaching style, and the coach will actually coach you for a short period of time.

When you hire a coach, it is important to ensure that you are fully committed to participating to get the most benefit out of the relationship. If you are truly dedicated to changing or growing in some area of your life, a coach will help you get there. Many people also have different coaches for different things. Some people have transformational coaches to help them transform their lives, some have health and fitness coaches to help them with their mindset around their health, and others have career coaches to assist them in with their career. There are coaches out there for almost anything, who can help strengthen your mentality in any aspect of your life or breakthrough what is holding you back. Do your research and search for reputable coaches in your area. They definitely shouldn't be hard to find.

The International Coaches Federation and the International Association of Coaching (Consider footnotes these with the websites) are governing bodies of the coaching profession. You can search for trained or certified coaches on their websites. Working with a coach is a big commitment, however, it can have a huge impact on your life, helping you get unstuck, find more happiness, or live your dreams. It is something worth exploring at the very least. Start by finding a coach and setting up a free sample session. If you are truly committed to getting unstuck and changing your life, your coach will help you see tremendous changes in your life. Think of the successful person you know, regardless of what they do, and chances are they have a life coach or life coaches helping them realize their potential and live their dreams.

FIFTH KEY: YOUR LIFE SUPPORT NETWORK

TRY THIS

Download and complete the **Life Support Network** worksheet

Learn more about coaching and how it can help you on your personal change journey; you can find out more about my coaching at www.iamDannyStone.com

You can get these downloadable worksheets at
www.YouHaveTheKeysNowDrive.com/resources

CHAPTER 6

FIRST HABIT: ESTABLISH A MORNING RITUAL

> *"The key to forming good habits is to make them part of your 'rituals.' I have a morning ritual, afternoon ritual, and Sunday ritual. It's one way to bundle good habits into regular times that you set aside to prepare yourself for the life you want. Rituals help you form habits."*
>
> –Lewis Howes

WHAT'S THE difference between you and someone who has the level of success that you desire? Their habits and the way they start their day! Successful people have more that morning routines – they have morning rituals You probably want to know the difference between a morning routine and morning ritual. A morning routine consists of all of the tasks that you have to do to start your day: shower, make your bed, brush your teeth, eat, and other necessary activities. They are not things you usually look forward to, however, you must do these things before getting your day started. Your morning ritual consists of activities that you look forward to every morning. They are sacred. Your ritual is what you do to set up your day for success and put you in a powerful, positive state of mind. If you want to become successful and have more peace, less stress and more happiness; a good place to start is by developing a morning ritual.

In studying highly successful people and people who are extremely happy and generous, I found two things that they have in common: they all have a morning ritual and they all have a bedtime routine. Successful people wake up early, usually between 4:30 and 6:00 in the morning and they complete a series of habits that they go through to form their morning ritual.

I'm sure you have heard of a guy by the name of Tony Robbins. If not, you need to hit up your friend Google and search his name.

Tony is the top peak performance coach in the world. He is the coach to celebrities, athletes, CEOs, Presidents of countries, and billionaires. Everyone from Serena Williams to Bill Clinton has called upon his wisdom to help them achieve their biggest goals and unlock more fulfillment in their lives.

Tony also has a documentary on Netflix called, **I Am Not Your Guru**. It is definitely worth watching.

I am going to tell you a secret, I was not always a fan of Tony. His in your face, bold, brash approach to helping people shift their mindset and take action was confusing and strange to me. I didn't understand it.

At first, I chose not to follow his work or listen to his audios or videos. Then something changed. I decided that I couldn't form an opinion about Tony without actually diving into his work a little more. I mean, he obviously he got results for his clients, he is the top peak performance coach in the world. I started watching his YouTube videos, listening to his audios and reading his books. As I did, I began to understand not only his extreme passion to help people live successful, meaningful lives but also why he coaches and ignites audiences the way he does. What Tony understands is that you have to disrupt a person's thinking and habits to help them change their lives. *You have to do something different if you want different results.* This is true for anyone, including you. If you are not where you want to be in your life, in your health, as a parent, in your career, financially, mentally, spiritually, or any area of importance - you must do something different!

What must be different to unlock true happiness and success?

Your habits!

Even more specifically, your morning habits, or as I describe them, your morning ritual. How you wake up every day will determine your level of success.

In his speech to a graduating class at Stanford, Steve Jobs said,

> "For the past 33 years, I have looked in the mirror every morning and asked myself: 'If today were the last day of my life, would I want to do what I am about to do today?"

FIRST HABIT: ESTABLISH A MORNING RITUAL

What a powerful way to start each day. We obviously know Jobs was one of the founders and former CEO of Apple. He revolutionized computer technology, the Smartphone, and how we listen to music, just to name a few of his accomplishments. He was truly someone determined to simplify technology and connect people around the world.

When you start each morning working on yourself and making sure that you are at your best, everything changes. Deciding that you are going to wake up and do the things that will change your life, that will move your life forward the most; is life-changing. Successful people know this. That's why they wake up early and take care of themselves and their goals first before they do anything else.

If you want more success, happiness, peace, a deeper spiritual connection, or have major goals you want to achieve, you must change your morning ritual. But wait! First, you have to develop a morning ritual.

I didn't know what a morning ritual was until I began to study personal development leaders and successful people. That is when my eyes were opened to how some people achieved amazing things in their lives. How did Princess Diana capture the attention of the world? How did Muhammad Ali become the most recognized person on the planet at one time? How did Nelson Mandela go from prisoner to president?

I had to study the greats if I wanted to become great and that is what I did and continue to do. What I realized is that almost all successful people have a morning ritual. They set up their days, weeks, months, and years for success based on the activities they do each morning. Of course, each ritual differs, however, there are certain activities that I found to be instrumental to personal change.

I call them 8 M's.

THEY ARE:

1. Meaning (gratitude)

2. Meditation

3. Mantra (affirmation)

4. Movement (exercise)
5. Meals
6. Massive goal actions
7. More personal development
8. Meaningful Journaling

If you can learn to master these 8 activities (the 8 Ms) you will master your life. Many of these are habits within themselves such as personal development or exercise, however, when you combine them together and take action before your day starts, you will get more done. It's not about simply getting more done, it's about doing the right things that are going to move you closer to mastery. It's about putting yourself, your desires, and your health and wellness first.

Let me give you a breakdown of each one:

MEANING (GRATITUDE)

Waking up in gratitude is the best way to start your day on a positive vibe. It's also one of the best ways to set up your day for success. When you focus on what you have and the things going right in your life, that's what you attract. When you focus on your problems and challenges they become amplified. Waking up with meaning and giving thanks is one of the most powerful things you can do to shift your mindset.

According to HappierHuman.com[1] being grateful has tons of benefits. They listed 7 categories with 31 benefits. This list of benefits was compiled by aggregating the results of more than 40 research studies on gratitude. Think of times when you have been grateful and see if any of these resonate with you. Table 6.1 shows the full list.

What a pretty incredible list, right? Who would have thought that there were so many benefits to being grateful? What does this mean for you? It means that when you start each morning in gratitude, you welcome many of these benefits into your life. How do you start each

---

[1] http://happierhuman.com/the-science-of-gratitude/

FIRST HABIT: ESTABLISH A MORNING RITUAL

GENERAL		EMOTIONAL	
1.	Makes us happier	2.	More Resilience
3.	Makes people like us	4.	More Good Feeling
5.	Healthier	6.	Happier Memories
7.	Boosts our careers	8.	Less Envy
9.	Strengthen our emotions	10.	More Relaxed
PERSONALITY		**SOCIAL**	
11.	More Optimistic	12.	More Friendly
13.	Less Materialistic	14.	Better Marriage
15.	More Spiritual	16.	More Respect
17.	Less Self-Centered	18.	More Friends
19.	More Self-Esteem	20.	Deeper Relationships
HEALTH		**CAREER**	
21.	Better Sleep	22.	Better Management
23.	Keeps The Doctor Away	24.	Increased Networking
25.	Longevity	26.	Goal Achievement
27.	More Energy	28.	Improved Decision Making
29.	More Exercise	30.	Increased Productivity
		31.	Better Management

Table 6.1: *Benefits of being grateful*

morning in meaning (gratitude)? As soon as you wake up, think of three things you are grateful for. You can write them down if you really want to dive into it. You can also think of and write down more if you like. The awesome thing about starting your day this way and writing them down is you wake up in a positive frame of mind setting the tone for the rest of your day. Writing them down allows you to document your gratitude for that day and allows you to go back and revisit the list later. Try it for at least a week and see what happens? See if you can detect any patterns? See if you notice a shift in your perspective/energy?

MEDITATION

Meditation can be intimidating for many people. Maybe it is for you. I know I used to be close-minded when it came to meditation. Mostly because I didn't understand the benefits and I didn't know what meditation really was. Meditation is simply taking quiet time to focus your thoughts and relax your mind to achieve mental and emotional clarity. It only requires you to find a quiet place, sit comfortably, take a few deep breaths, close your eyes and focus on your breathing. You can do this in only 3-5 minutes. That's not so bad, is it?

Of course, there are different types of meditations. Some meditations have chanting, some are done in conjunction with yoga or other fitness activities, however, that is basic meditation. I talk more about meditation in Chapter 9. What you need to know to start with is that taking time each morning to calm your mind, to think deeply, to sit quietly, is very important to your mental, physical and spiritual health. You can even sit quietly with your cup of coffee or smoothie and meditate. Or, put on a calming song and relax while you take in the sounds. There are no rules as to how to meditate other than to sit, be still, and clear your mind. Try it for a few days and see how you feel. See what it opens up for you.

MANTRA (AFFIRMATION)

A mantra is a powerful statement, a set of words or a chant that you repeat to yourself to increase your concentration and tap into your personal power. Sometimes mantras are said while meditating or doing yoga, however, mantras can be used separately. I often recommend that you develop your mantra and say it to yourself when you are looking in the mirror or while starting your day. When you look in the mirror and recite your mantra statement to yourself over and over, day after day, you will begin to believe it. You will begin to feel the words and then live them. Does it sound too simple? Does it sound too easy to be true? Well, mantras and affirmations have been around for a thousand years and many cultures and religions make reference to the power of chanting mantras to oneself. Think about what you say to and about yourself right now. Do you speak highly of yourself? Do you speak to yourself in strong, positive words? Or do you talk down to yourself? Do you have a lot of self-doubts and negative self-talk? You are what you say you are, and that's why it is important to begin your day speaking about your amazing qualities or tapping into a higher connection. Try it, what's the worst that can happen?

MOVEMENT (EXERCISE)

This is nothing new to you I am sure, however, I will tell you again, and I will tell you again later on chapter 9, exercise regularly. But you already know this. Maybe you already do exercise regularly; if so, that's awesome. If you don't, then it's time to start. I'm sure you know all of the health benefits to exercising, however, it can never be said enough. What activities are you consistently doing to maintain your health and overall well-being? Are you walking, jogging, biking, hiking, going to the gym, doing at-home workouts, playing on sports teams, running around with your children, walking your dog, gardening? What are you doing? And, how often are you doing it? Once a week? Twice? Three times? I am the first person to tell you that exercising can be challenging because you may lack motivation, time, and effort. By thinking about the benefits of exercise it will help shift your mindset around being active. Also, exercising in the morning before you begin your day reduces the chance of your busy scheduling hindering you from being active later on in the day or evening. It is also the best time for your body. Your body is primed and ready to get going in the morning and morning exercise is just what it needs to kick start your day. The awesome thing about morning movement is that you can burn calories and get your heart rate up with only a minimum of 10 minutes per day. Find some free online videos and do an at-home workout, run around the block, get out in your back yard or do some type of exercise. Your body will thank you.

MEALS

You are what you eat. I'm sure you have heard this before. You can fuel your body or your vehicle with regular fuel or with premium, high octane fuel. Which one will give you a bigger boost? Your body is your temple and when you feed your body, you feed your mind and spirit. There are many studies that state when a person begins their day with a healthy meal it not only benefits their body but also has positive effects on their mindset. When you eat a healthy breakfast in the morning you are more alert, think more clearly, and improve your concentration.

Developing a healthy lifestyle contributes to overall health and weight loss. In your pursuit of more happiness and success, your diet is a major factor to ensure you have the energy and focus to see your goals through. This is something that is overlooked by many people including those who have achieved a certain level of success. Some of the most successful people in the world neglect their diets and do not start their day with healthy meals. As a result, they eventually have health issues. I have witnessed this first hand with coaching clients, family, friends, and coworkers. I have also experienced this personally. I never used to eat breakfast. I would jump up out of bed, hit the gym or do some personal development activities, grab a banana or something then go to work. It began to catch up with me throughout the day and eventually I realized that I lacked energy and concentration. I never had the energy or focus to chase my goals and dreams. When I finally started eating a healthy breakfast, that's when my energy levels, focus, and work ethic increased. Are you eating a healthy breakfast? Do you have a meal ritual that you look forward to in the morning? Maybe it's your oatmeal or cup of coffee, or maybe you love making your delicious morning smoothie. Whatever it is, wake up and get going on your premium fuel for your body.

MASSIVE GOAL ACTIONS

You need to become a goal-getter! If you have major goals that you want to achieve, the morning is the best time to map out your plan or take action if possible. Each morning you should write down your goals and your most important tasks for your goals. Decide which 3-4 actions are most important and do those as soon as possible. If you cannot do those tasks in the morning, then schedule them into your day to ensure that you knock them off for the day. What many people don't realize is that our dreams are a compilation of smaller goals and even smaller daily actions. If you have big goals that you want to achieve you have to be consistent in your daily actions and do the most important tasks every day.

Each day you get closer and closer to what may seem impossible. I talk more about goals and give you a simple goal plan in Chapter 8.

What you need to know is that every single day when you wake up, you need to write down your tasks for the day, take action on them, and track your progress.

MORE PERSONAL DEVELOPMENT

Read more books, watch more personal development videos, listen to more podcasts, take more courses, listen to audios! Do more personal development if you want personal change. Okay, I'm done. I'm joking, but you get my point. Why is it that many of us spend time on career development and very little time on our personal development? You deserve more out of life and the way to get more - knowledge, love, money, better mental health, and anything else you desire, is to spend time working on you. What areas of your life need more attention? If you cannot think of anything refer back to the Wheel of Life exercise. about that. Whatever areas you need to devote more attention to you have the ability to learn more about building yourself up in those areas.

Find books on relationships if you are having some challenges in your relationship. Watch self-help videos or listen to podcasts if you need motivation. Find online chat groups if you need support in certain areas of your life. It's like everything else in your morning ritual, make the time as soon as you can to make your personal development a priority. When you take care of yourself first, you are better equipped to care for those around you. Think about reading a few chapters of a book each morning, listening to a podcast watching a YouTube video, or taking an online course. Think about developing a routine/ritual that works for you. Experiment/challenge yourself. What can you do for 10 to 20 minutes each day to develop yourself? What can you do that will move your closer to crush your goals and dreams?

MINDFUL JOURNALING

Journaling is a great way to capture your thoughts, emotions and perspective. Writing can help you gain clarity, emphasize gratitude and organize your goals. There is lots of research around the benefits of journaling. It can increase your IQ and emotional intelligence. It can help you boost your memory and increase your communication.

It can help you build your self-confidence and even spark creativity. There is power in putting pen to paper.

I'll be honest with you, I never considered myself much of a writer. I definitely never thought I would be an author. It all changed one morning when I woke up and just wrote down some thoughts, the next day I wrote more thoughts and so on and so on until it became a part of my morning ritual. Make journaling a part of your morning ritual. Keep a pen and notepad by your bed and as you wake up, write down whatever comes to mind. Maybe you want to write down things you are grateful for, or your tasks for the day, or how you are feeling. It doesn't matter what it is, just write. Something will begin to shift within you when you review your journal and reflect on your thoughts and activities over time. It's almost like you are seeing the movie of your life play out on paper. Think about how interesting that would be.

When I established a morning ritual, my life shifted. My confidence increased, I had more peace and calm in my life, I had more clarity, my mental and physical health increased, and I began to crush goals I never thought were possible. I know what you are thinking… "Danny, you did all of this by doing a few things in the morning?" my answer is YES! You may be also thinking… "I don't have time to do all of these things in the morning" That's a valid point as well. You don't have the luxury of NOT doing this.

What if I told you that you can customize your morning ritual to fit YOUR needs. And, what if I told you that your morning ritual only requires 30 to 60 minutes of your time? Think about it, you can change your life, achieve your biggest goals, and unlock more clarity in your life by incorporating a morning ritual that takes only 30 minutes a day.

I had been doing my morning ritual for a while and I noticed a huge shift within me. I had more energy, focus, and clarity. I knew it was working for me so I began to share it with friends and coaching clients and it worked for them too. They began to see similar results and that's when I knew I had to share it with more people. The question is, will a morning ritual help you on your journey to personal change? The answer is yes! It will work for you too, if you decide to do something different. If you truly want personal change, if you want to be more

FIRST HABIT: ESTABLISH A MORNING RITUAL

confident or achieve your biggest goals, you must commit to personal development. What you put into yourself you get out of yourself.

I came across a book called the **Miracle Morning** by Hal Elrod. It's a great book that really teaches you how to set up your days, weeks, months and years for success. In the book Hal says something that really resonates with me, he said,

> *"We all want Level 10 success, in all areas of our lives – health, happiness, finances, relationships, career, spirituality, you name it – but if our level of personal development (knowledge, experience, mindset, beliefs, etc.) in any given area not at Level 10, then life is always going to be a struggle. Our outer world will always be a reflection of our inner world. Our level of success is always going to parallel our level of personal development. Until we dedicate time each day to developing ourselves into the person we need to create the life we want, success is always going to be a struggle."*

I'm no diver but that's deep! (bad joke I know). However, Hal is completely right. None of us will ever achieve the success and happiness we want in our lives if we don't put in the personal development work. If we don't wake up with the mindset that we are on a journey to achieve what we want we will never get what we want. We must be dedicated to a morning ritual – to beginning each day in action.; Action that will move our lives to a place that we never thought possible. I believe you can become the person you desire to become. I believe you have the ability to live the life you want if you put in the work. And the interesting thing about it is that you can change your life by simply dedicating 30-60 minutes at the start of each day to your morning ritual. emerged in the most important habits. Whether your morning ritual is the 8Ms I discussed earlier or you develop your own ritual, dedicate time to waking up early and practicing your morning ritual.

This is a sample morning ritual. If you cannot do all of these things then do what you can. If you only have 20 minutes then do what you think will benefit you the most to ensure you set your day up for success. If you find that you want to practice doing all of these things but don't have time, try waking up an extra 30 minutes earlier. It may be difficult for the first week, however, after that you will find it easier to wake up earlier and you will begin to look forward to waking up early to get going on your morning ritual. The main take away is to wake up a little earlier and do your morning ritual, whatever it looks like to you.

TRY THIS

Wake up 15 minutes early for a week, then 30 minutes earlier the next week

Do the morning ritual for the next week, you can pick 4 of the habits to take action on or you can do all of them or you can create your own morning ritual

Share your thoughts in the **Driver of Your Destiny** community on Facebook

Share your morning ritual posts on Instagram, Twitter or Facebook and tag me @iamDannyStone

Commit to trying out the morning ritual for 30 days

You can get these downloadable worksheets at
www.YouHaveTheKeysNowDrive.com/resources

CHAPTER 7

SECOND HABIT: DEVELOP A BEDTIME ROUTINE

"The way to a more productive, more inspired, more joyful life is getting enough sleep."
–Arianna Huffington

SLEEP. Many people want more of it and all of us want a better quality of sleep. Not getting enough sleep can result in you being irritable, not being able to focus, anxiety, health issues, increased stress, and chronic fatigue. Maybe you can relate. When you don't get a good night's rest do you experience any of these symptoms? Are you grumpy or short with people? Do you feel groggy and not sharp? Do you find your body feeling sluggish or do you find yourself gaining weight and you are not sure why? It may be that you are not getting the proper amount of rest and not getting quality sleep.

The other challenge with getting a night of good sleep is inconsistency in bedtimes. Going to bed at different times can throw off your internal alarm. It confuses your body and throws off your mental state. Have you ever slept for 8 or 9 hours and woke up feeling like you hadn't slept at all? Or have you gone to bed at different times and felt like your mental awareness was lacking? That's the downside of not getting quality sleep.

There are tons of resources out there to help us get a better night's rest: high tech beds, sleep machines, sound machines, sleep meditations, blackout masks, Smartphone apps and more. With all of these resources we should be getting better quality sleep. However, most people would agree that they are not. Two questions to ask yourself are "why can't I get a better night's sleep?" and "how does getting a better sleep enhance my productivity, my ability to deal with stress, and build my confidence?"

It's time to talk about your sleep habits.

Over the last few years sleep has been a hot topic. There has been lots of research on sleep and sleep disorders, best-selling books, new sleep products, and even sleep coaches all devoted to helping you sleep more soundly. But what does a better sleep have to do with you getting what you want in life? ALOT!

Highly successful people have known about the importance of sleep for years! They know that in order to function at a high level they need to start setting up their day the night before, and that means getting both the right amount of sleep and good quality of sleep. I remember when I was working for an organization managing all their training and employee development. It was a very demanding job and I often worked somewhat long hours. While I was working full-time I also had my consulting business on the side and I was doing lots of work in the community with youth. My plate was "full" and I was not getting quality sleep. I would sleep only 4.5 to 5 hours a night and it was not good quality sleep. Boy, would I feel it sometimes! I was always tired. At times I couldn't think clearly. Once in a while, I would be short with people, and I couldn't focus on important topics. I knew I was not getting enough sleep and the quality of sleep that I was getting was very poor. I knew I couldn't continue along that path because if I did, eventually I would burn out and that could have led to my body shutting down or other major health issues.

What did I do? I changed my bedtime routine. Wait, let me be honest, I *developed* a bedtime routine, I never really had one before. My goal was to go to bed around the same time every night. The TV and electronic devices were shut off half an hour before I went to bed. I followed the same hygiene routine and I made notes about what I wanted to accomplish the next day. It was also important for me to aim to wake up at the same time every morning. Now, this didn't happen overnight, but after 6? Weeks, I had a new routine and could see and feel the difference. What changed for me is that I woke up with more energy and focus. I was clear about my day and most importantly I got better quality sleep.

What I realized was, is that in order to be at my best and to wear all of the hats I had to wear every day, it was important for me to have

SECOND HABIT: DEVELOP A BEDTIME ROUTINE

a bedtime routine and get quality sleep. Since then I have been curious about the importance of sleep and the sleep habits of highly successful people.

In my research, I found that successful people incorporate various practices into their nighttime routines. If you want more energy, clarity, better health and better quality sleep, maybe you can adopt some of these practices into your bedtime routine.

HERE ARE 10 SLEEP PRACTICES OF SUCCESSFUL PEOPLE:

1. They know the ideal number of hours of sleep they need to perform at their optimal levels
2. They have the same hygiene regime every night
3. They go to bed at the same time every night, even on weekends
4. They turn off all electronic devices before bed
5. They read or write before lights out
6. They jot down 2-3 things they want to accomplish the next day
7. They create the right ambiance with complete darkness and ambient sounds
8. They wake up early
9. They wake up at the same time every day, even on weekends
10. keep the temperature in the room cool

What is your bedtime routine? Do you have a consistent nightly routine before you go to sleep? It is important for you to develop your own personal routine to help you wind down, set up your night for optimal sleep, and wake up recharged and refreshed.

If you feel like you don't have energy during the day, if you feel irritable, or you just feel a bit unbalanced, then you may need better quality sleep. A night of better quality sleep doesn't mean more hours, it means that you wake up well-rested and ready to begin your day. There's often a big misconception about more hours of sleep being equivalent to better quality sleep. That's not true. In fact, Dr. Michael

Breus, known as The Sleep Doctor, one of the foremost sleep experts in the world, says 8 hours sleep is not the ideal number for everyone. The National Sleep Foundation agrees, they came out with a report that identifies targeted sleep numbers by age range. It breaks down sleep recommendations into nine age-specific categories with a range for each, which allows for individual differences:

- Older adults, 65+ years: 7-8 hours
- Adults, 26-64 years: 7-9 hours
- Young adults, 18-25 years: 7-9 hours
- Teenagers, 14-17 years: 8-10 hours
- School-age children, 6-13 years: 9-11 hours
- Preschool children, 3-5 years: 10-13 hours
- Toddlers, 1-2 years: 11-14 hours
- Infants, 4-11 months: 12-15 hours
- Newborns, 0-3 months: 14-17 hours

As you can see, there is no longer that "you need 8 hours of sleep to give your body the proper amount of rest" theory. Instead, there are various ranges of sleep based on age ranges. What does this mean for you? The amount of sleep you need will vary between a range depending on your age. And if you get the proper amount of quality sleep it should provide your body and your mind with the ability to function at your expected level. A minimum of 7 hours of sleep is a step in the right direction.

However, it's not just about sleep! Your bedtime routine has a lot to do with you getting the quality sleep you need and setting up the next day for success. How you prepare for bed has a lot to do with how you wake up. A good bedtime routine means you are priming your mind and body for sleep and to recharge and rejuvenate itself during the night. Research suggests you take 30-60 minutes to wind down for sleep. Switching off electronics or closing down all social media, reading, meditation, listening to music, and writing can help put you in the right sleep mindset. It will calm your mind and body and quiet your active mind. Adjusting the temperature in your bedroom, having comfortable pillows, and making sure the room is completely dark may help you to get to sleep quicker.

Even making sure that you brush your teeth and wash your face at the same time will lock you in for a night of good sleep. Whatever your routine, be consistent. Begin your bedtime routine at the same time and go to bed at the same time every night. In the morning wake up at the same time.

EXERCISE #1: BEDTIME ROUTINE

Create your own bedtime routine. Try to go to bed at the same time and wake up at the same time for 7 days. On a piece of paper or in your Smartphone notes, write down the following.

1. The amount of sleep I need is _____
2. I will go to bed _____ every night for the next 7 nights
3. I will wake up at _____ every morning for the next 7 days
4. My bedtime routine will consist of
   a) _____
   b) _____
   c) _____
   d) _____
   e) _____
   f) _____

Make this commitment for the next 7 nights and see how you feel. Start your wind down for sleep 30 minutes before you are set to go to bed. Turn off your devices and start to relax your mind. When you get a night of good quality sleep you will enhance all areas of your life.

> **TRY THIS**
>
> Go to www.YouHaveTheKeysNowDrive/resources to download the free sleep exercise.
>
> Commit to doing your bedtime routine for at least 7 days
>
> Share your thoughts in the Driver of Your Destiny community
>
> Share posts of your routine on social media and tag me on Instagram, Twitter and Facebook using the tag @iamDannyStone

You can get these downloadable worksheets at
www.YouHaveTheKeysNowDrive.com/resources

CHAPTER 8

THIRD HABIT: GET GOING ON YOUR GOALS

"Your goals are the road maps that guide you and show you what is possible for your life."
—Les Brown

Knowing what you want in life is a great feeling. It is definitely an important step in the process of being successful. If you are one of the lucky few who knows what you want, then ask yourself, "What do I need to do to achieve what I want?" and "What steps should I take to reach my end goal?" Setting goals is important because it allows you to monitor your progress and fully experience your successes. If you don't have goals, how will you change your life? How will you accomplish what you want? Without goals, how is it possible to get unstuck? The simple answer is: it's not. Granted, sometimes life will happen and you will be the recipient of what you want in life because you attract things. You could buy a lottery ticket and become an instant millionaire; however, to be who you want to be and live how you want to live, you must set goals for yourself.

The website StaticBrain analyzed New Year's goals and found that just eight percent of those surveyed achieved their goals while ninety-two percent did not. Based on this data, most people don't achieve their goals that they set at the beginning of the year. The question is, why not? An even bigger question is why don't most people achieve their goals in general? I believe there are a number of reasons, however, I will give you my top ten reasons.

11 reasons I believe people do not achieve their goals:

1. They are unclear on what they truly want to achieve
2. They have a fear of success or failure

3. They procrastinate and lack motivation
4. They have no real plan
5. They let other people sabotage their progress
6. They have too many
7. They do not truly want the change
8. They do not take action on their goals every day
9. They cannot visually see themselves achieving their goals
10. They were not successful in the past
11. They never get started

Do any of these reasons sound familiar to you? There are other reasons, of course, but these seem to be the most common. I did not list these reasons to help you justify why you are not achieving your goals. This list is not to provide you with excuses. It is merely to show you that in order to ensure you are successfully completing your goals, you have to be aware of roadblocks that you will likely encounter so that you can combat them and find ways around them.

Tony Robbins, the self-help and life-coach guru says that in order to successfully achieve your goals and have a lasting change, you must look at your goals from a "must perspective" instead of a "should perspective." When you think about things that you "should do," whether you think you should lose weight, you should find a new job, or you should buy a home, you will find a way to *not* make it real. You will allow excuses to justify why you do not achieve your goals.

However, if you change your perspective to "must do," you shift your thinking and take action because you see your goals and changing your life as things that you need to do. I completely agree with this principle. If you make something a priority, a must; you are more likely to achieve it than if it is something you should do, or would like to do; maybe, one day, when the time is right. You have to be excited about what achieving your goals gives you; you need to have passion and determination to ruthlessly go after what you want.

THIRD HABIT: GET GOING ON YOUR GOALS

You cannot go through life without setting meaningful goals. Well, you can, but you just don't accomplish nearly as much. There are things that you want to achieve in life and each one requires a plan and action. In my experience working with hundreds of people to achieve their goals, most people do not set effective goals. Most people say that they want to accomplish or achieve something, yet they do not set true goals with action plans.

Here's an example: Have you ever set a goal to take a trip somewhere that you have always wanted to travel to and you still have not gone? What held you back from taking that trip at the time? What is holding you back now? Let me guess; money, family obligations, your job, not enough time? Does this sound familiar? I agree that there are many obstacles; I get that you have many responsibilities and sometimes you have to put your goals on hold.

What I also know is that anything is possible if you have determination, motivation, and you set effective goals. I am not talking about a goal like, "One day, I am going to travel to France and see the Eiffel Tower." The problem with this goal is that it is too vague; there is no time frame, and no action plan to make this happen. Instead of a goal, it is a wish and possibly a want. I say possibly because if you truly wanted something, you would put forth the effort to achieve it and it would include a plan.

Successful people set goals and achieve their goals because they take action; they do something every day that will drive them closer to success. They don't allow obstacles to deflate their determination to achieve their goals. Sure, they encounter challenges along the way; some may even fail many, many times, yet they stay the course and find a way to win. A part of their reason for success is that they set goals and look at them from a "must" perspective. There are also other factors: they have a support system, they are willing to step outside their comfort zone, and they continue to challenge themselves. In the end, they take action; they do something. You can take action too. You can set goals and dedicate yourself to achieving them.

Traditional goal setting can be effective; however, future-forward goal setting is a lot more effective. Future forward goal setting is envisioning and behaving from the standpoint of already having achieved your goal. You flash forward to actually achieving your goal and develop a reverse plan. You back up the actions that drove you to success and establish what needs to be done to get there. Aside from various online goal planning systems and models, there are goal-setting applications for your mobile devices to help keep you on track as well. You can search for goal-setting applications on your mobile device to see what is available.

GET A GOAL PLAN

I am not one for complicated, time-consuming goal plans. They don't work for me because I end up spending more time trying to figure out the plan and writing it out then I do actually taking action. In order to achieve your goals, you have to have a simple, actionable plan that holds you accountable for doing what you set out to do. This is why I created a Goal Setting Blueprint. It is an easy to follow, step-by-step strategy to help you crush your goals. The reason why so many of my clients and myself have achieved major goals in our lives is that we have used this simple strategy to help change our goal achievement mindset and take massive actions. The blueprint consists of three parts, two of which I have never seen in a plan before, your success and failure patterns.

The Blueprint is a three-step process. In Step One, you look at your success patterns. You take time to reflect on times when you have been successful in the past. You identify actions, attitudes, behaviours, and people who helped you achieve major goals in the past. Once you compare your major goals you will see similar actions that you have taken in the past to get you across the finish line. I call this your "success pattern." You will use this to set and achieve your current and future goals.

Step Two is your failure patterns, you guessed it! You will look at major goals you did not achieve in the past and the things that have held you back. You will avoid these things in the future. Maybe you shared your goals with people who were not supportive and they talked you out of your goals. Maybe you didn't take action on your goals daily or maybe.

There are many goal setting tools out there. If you search the internet or mobile applications you will find plenty. The most important thing is to find one that you believe will work for you. In the simplest form, write down your specific goal, the steps you will take daily, weekly, or monthly, consider roadblocks you will encounter along the way, think about the support that you need to be successful, and put a time-frame on it. Also, be sure to have milestones and celebrations along the way to keep you motivated. Decide who you will share your goals with and how you will celebrate.

Regardless of the goal plan you choose, it is important to write out your goals, post them where you can see them, and monitor your progress on a regular basis. If you utilize a goal-planning model, you will increase your chances of moving forward and achieving your goals. Remember, it is easier to change and adapt your plan when you actually have a plan. This is not to say that your life should revolve around strict plans, tasks, and goals. I do believe sometimes people have to allow things to manifest themselves; however, a plan confirms your commitment to yourself.

BE VISUAL

People think in images. We have a natural ability to visualize and symbolize ideas and goals. We communicate in imagery. It is how we relate to each other and everything around us. Using imagery when setting your goals can be very powerful. In fact, many successful people utilize visuals and visualization techniques to help them achieve their goals. Visualizing your success is a powerful way to actualize your success. Seeing your success on a daily basis helps your mind to work subconsciously towards what you want in life.

One example of a being visual is a vision or goal board. This is a foam board, corkboard, or even just a place on a wall where you put pictures of your goals, dreams, and role models. The images or words on your board represent what you want in life. Seeing these images on a daily basis will motivate you to take action. When you dedicate a space in your home or workspace to visual representations of what you want in life, it allows the universe to hear you, your inner self to take action, and your goals will become more real to you.

Another way to incorporate visuals into achieving your goals is to utilize visualization techniques. Many athletes, CEOs, entertainers, and successful business people utilize visualization techniques to help them excel in the achievement of their goals. Jim Carrey, a world-famous comedian, and actor, believes in the power of visualization. He has long told the story of writing himself a check for $10 million dollars well before he was rich and famous. He postdated the cheque for 1995 and carried it in his wallet. Carrey would also visualize cashing the check and buying items with the money. When 1995 hit, he definitely had enough money to cash the check, yet he never did. Instead, he put it in his father's jacket after he passed away.

Michael Phelps is on record as being the most decorated Olympian of all time, with a record 22 medals: 18 gold, 2 silver, and 2 bronze. He claims visualization was and continues to be the secret to his success. Phelps claims that he has been visualizing the perfect swim since the age of seven! In an interview, he is quoted as saying:

> "I like to think of myself as a normal person who has a passion, has a goal and a dream and goes out and does it. Throughout my career, nobody has been able to stand in my way. I have gone through ups and downs. Nobody is going to put a limit on what I'm doing. I'm going to do what I want to do when I want to do it. That is how I have always worked. If I want something I am going to go and get it."

Phelps attributes his work ethic to dreaming big, setting goals, and visualizing his success at an early age. Phelps is a clear example that anyone, any age, anywhere, can visualize their success and make it a reality.

Though he became a highly successful athlete, he was not always at the top of his sport. Visualization techniques can work for anyone, as long as you are willing to see your goals and believe success is possible. Many life and executive coaches realize the power of visualization, which is why they utilize the technique with their clients. I will tell you a secret, anyone can visual their success. You don't have to be famous, a life coach, or have any training to do it. All you need is a vision of what you want and the dedication to envision it often, combined with taking action.

Here's how: think of a goal and consider what success looks like to you. Take some time to close your eyes and think about yourself achieving your goal. Take in all aspects of what is happening: the location, people, sounds, and smells, everything you can think of. You should do this on a daily basis, taking a few moments every day to visualize success. Eventually, you will subconsciously begin to take action towards your goal. It is not magic, it may not even work for you; however, as I stated, when we have strong connections with our goals, it creates a stronger bond to actualizing what we want to achieve.

By reflecting on what success looks and feels like on a daily basis, in conjunction with taking action daily, your chances of success increase tremendously.

SYMBOLS
Using symbols is another way to utilize the power of connection with your goals. Seeing, hearing, or holding something that is symbolic to you, something that has meaning in your journey to achieve your life goals can help immensely. Symbols are personal to you, which means they may not mean anything to anyone else, yet they are things that you can hold or see to remind you of what is important to you in life.

A symbol could be a picture of your children, partner, or loved ones. It could be a key chain that reminds you of a place you want to travel to or a special object that has significant meaning to you. Symbols are things that ignite your desire to continue to chase your goals with great determination. And, in times when you are unmotivated, symbols can re-energize you and re-ignite your fire to carry on.

Symbols can also motivate you to get out of a rut or jumpstart you from being stuck. They can be used to remind you of your values, passions, and purpose in life through difficult and trying times. Think of symbols you can utilize to help you stay on track. Carry those symbols with you on a daily basis. They can be things you carry in your wallet, in your pocket, or on your Smartphone, or possibly something that has a significant meaning that you can call upon when saboteurs show up, and they will.

Set goals and aspirations for yourself. Think about how you can achieve what you want in life. However, do not get caught up with the "how." Just start doing something NOW. Start visualizing your success and see where it takes you. See yourself doing what you love and visualize it often. Think of symbols that have a significant meaning to you and carry them with you. Incorporating visual techniques and symbols in your life will help you see what is possible and prepare you to step into your dreams when opportunities present themselves. They will also drive your success and take you to places you never knew were possible.

Do not be afraid to declare what you want; put it out there in the universe. The law of attraction states that you attract what you truly want. To be yourself, you have to see yourself. To be successful, you have to see your success. To find true love you must love yourself and see what true love looks like. If you consistently see it, feel it, sense it, and strive for it, you will be it and achieve it; whatever "it" is to you.

CELEBRATE WINS ALONG THE WAY

There is a great quote by Tom Peters, which speaks to the importance of celebrating your successes to encourage more success. He says...

"Celebrate what you want to see more of."

Setting and achieving goals is a long journey. There are many obstacles which can potentially deter people from continuing to see their goals through to the end. To reach your goals, you need to have determination and perseverance, as well as devoting time, effort, and sometimes money. It takes courage to step outside of your comfort zone and battle saboteurs to reach your end destination of success and happiness. It is important to celebrate wins along the way, and especially celebrate when you achieve your goals. Too often, people set goals and devote a tremendous amount of time and effort to achieving them, yet they do not celebrate along the way. Take time to reflect on your accomplishments and reward yourself for stepping up to do something that you set out to do.

Writing down your goals, monitoring your progress, keeping a checklist, and documenting milestones area all key to your success because they allow you to visually chart your progress. Seeing your achievements on paper will stimulate your desire to complete your goal. Sometimes, not having a well-thought-out plan, but just taking action can lead you to where you want to go. Regardless, celebrating your wins and sharing your experiences with others significantly increases your chances of achieving what you want in life.

Many people do not take time to enjoy success while on their journey to living their dreams. They are so focused on getting unstuck or achieving the ultimate goal that they do not think about enjoying the journey along the way. This is one reason people don't achieve what they set out to do.

When you do not celebrate along the way, you depriving yourself of the efforts needed to see your goal through. Experiencing your progress and sharing your wins with others gives you a taste of success and helps you focus on the finish line. Attempting to change your life or step outside of your comfort zone is a challenge. When you do, you need to reward yourself along the way to keep the momentum going and to give yourself a taste of success. Maybe not with huge rewards or celebrations, but; with simple or meaningful things like taking an hour for yourself, buying yourself a small gift, or treating yourself to a meal you enjoy. It is personal to you.

Like some of the best food in the world, you must marinate in your success. Do not rush into basking in the glory of your achievements. You owe it to yourself to take time to celebrate when you achieve what you want. One of the greatest feelings in the world is setting a goal, something that you truly want in life, and then actually achieving it. It is rewarding and satisfying to know that you have put forth so much effort, overcome many obstacles, and silenced the saboteurs (those voices and critics) to get to your end destination. Celebrating your success helps to program your subconscious to develop patterns to drive future success. You create a feeling and experience that you will want to achieve again and again and lock it in your mind.

When you take time to appreciate your journey and reward yourself, you are telling yourself that you are worthy of being successful. You are worthy of the benefits associated with achieving your goals. Your mind will lock in those emotions and feelings and use that as fuel for your next journey.

Enjoy your success and be sure to celebrate in whatever way you feel is appropriate for each goal you achieve. It can be as big or as small a celebration as you want. You may also want to include those in your Life Support Network connections the people who have supported you and held you accountable along the way. You could send a thank-you card or take them for lunch. You can take yourself to dinner, buy yourself something, write yourself a letter and post it on your wall, share with friends on social media, or take a trip. You can reward yourself any way you choose. The point is to take the time to reflect and enjoy success. To finally get to your end destination of achieving what you set out to achieve, you owe yourself the enjoyment of appreciating your journey. You are *the champ* and you can decide how to reward yourself for your victory.

One of the greatest, most well-known athletes of all time, Muhammad Ali, was known as the most prolific booster in sports. He would walk into press conferences with opponents and claim, "The champ is here" even when he was not the champion at the time. For him, it was a way to mentally throw off his opponent; however, it was also a way for him to pump himself up and prepare for what he thought would be a victory. It was his announcement to the world that he was the champion and proud to let others know.

I am not saying you should brag about your achievements and embellish your accomplishments. However, the lesson to be learned is that you **are** a champion. You are born to be successful and have great things happen in your life. And when you work hard to get unstuck or achieve your goals, you owe it to yourself, and those who supported you, to celebrate. Do not downplay your successes. Do not shy away from feeling great about your accomplishments and sharing them with others. Think like a champion, be a champion, and reward yourself

THIRD HABIT: GET GOING ON YOUR GOALS

like a champion. When you make life changes and do something that you have longed to do, which you have no doubt done at some point in your life, you are a champion and champions receive rewards and celebrate.

EXERCISE #1: SIMPLE GOAL PLAN

I want you to achieve your biggest goals. I want you to have experiences that you didn't even know were possible. To move you in the right direction you need a simple, yet effective goal plan. Putting everything together that I just mentioned in this chapter, here is a simple goal plan that will help you crush your goals.

1. On a few pieces of blank paper here is what you are going to do. At the top, write Your Name and The Date

2. Make a list of all your goals right now

3. Put a checkmark next to the goal that will move your life forward the most right now. This is the goal you will make a plan for (you can repeat this for other goals)

4. Write down why this goal is important to you

5. Set a deadline. When do you want to accomplish this goal by? (you can always adjust the deadline, but you need something to work towards)

6. Break the goal down into 3-4 smaller chunks (milestones)

7. If your bigger deadline is a 1-year timeline to accomplish your goal, break it down into smaller goals every 3-4 months

8. Write down how you will celebrate each milestone and how you will celebrate completing bigger goals

9. List all the tasks that you must accomplish to reach each milestone and your bigger goal

10. Organize the list in terms of importance, what do you need to achieve first, second, third, fourth, etc.

11. Make a list of potential challenges and how you will get through them

12. List your Life Support Network, the people you will tell about this goal and who will support you

13. Enter your goal in your calendar or Smartphone on the date you selected as your deadline

14. Get going on your goals! Wake up every day and decide on

15. your top 3 most important tasks and do the most important tasks first

16. Monitor your progress

17. Keep going until you WIN!

This is a simple goal plan you can use to help you organize your goals and take action on the most important goals you have right now. The most important thing about achieving any goal is to take **consistent, daily** action. Making this a part of your morning ritual will help you focus and keep you acting on your goals. If you cannot take action in the morning, find some other time in the day to do something towards your goals. You will be surprised at the progress you will make by doing at least one thing daily. It's time to become a goal-getter!

    If you need more help and want to take your goal-achievement to the next level, you can check out my Success Mindset Goal-Setting Blueprint on my website: www.iamDannyStone.com I dive deeper into how to achieve your goals and walk you through the goal-setting system that my clients and I use to achieve our BIGGEST goals. The thing to remember is to get started. Take action. You can always develop and revise your plan along the way, however, getting started is more important than waiting for the perfect time or having the perfect plan.

THIRD HABIT: GET GOING ON YOUR GOALS

TRY THIS

Do this **Simple Goal Plan**

Learn more about goal-setting at
www.iamDannyStone.com

Join the Driver of Your Destiny community on Facebook and share your goals, progress and ask questions

---

You can get these downloadable worksheets at
www.YouHaveTheKeysNowDrive.com/resources

CHAPTER 9

FOURTH HABIT: MIND YOUR FITNESS AND SPIRIT

> *"Women, in particular, need to keep an eye on their physical and mental health, because if we're scurrying to and from appointments and errands, we don't have a lot of time to take care of ourselves. "We need to do a better job of putting ourselves higher on our own 'to-do' list."*
> —Michelle Obama

YOU NEED a 'time out!' No, I am not talking about the punishment you give to your children when they are misbehaving. I am talking about taking time for yourself. In the midst of trying to discover your true self, live your life purpose, achieve your life goals, live your life and connect with loved ones, it is also important to take time out for yourself. Life is busy. There is always a lot going on, which is why it is so important to slow down and focus on you.

Taking care of yourself, mentally, physically, and spiritually, is one of the best things that you can do to help you focus and rise to the challenge of truly unleashing your greatness. You need to take time to reflect, meditate, and ponder the things that happen in your daily life.

Life moves fast. Remember high school? Your child's first steps? Your first job? Well, maybe you don't remember all of that, but my point is, some things in life seem as though they just happened yesterday when in fact it has been years since they have passed. In the midst of living busy lives, we need to stop to truly understand ourselves, to connect with who we truly are and to connect with? Find our place in? the universe.

Knowing who you are is important, but continuing to connect with yourself, your thoughts, and the universe is just as important. Take time to pause, reflect, meditate, be physically active, anything that allows you to connect with your inner thoughts, emotions, and energy.

THE POWER OF MEDITATION

If you do not know what meditation is, let me explain. Meditation can be defined as a practice where an individual focuses their mind on a particular object, thought, or activity to achieve a mentally clear and emotionally calm state. It is simply taking quiet time for yourself to connect with who you are and develop a state of consciousness and awareness. It helps to build internal energy, relaxation, and a deeper understanding of yourself and everything around you. It helps you center yourself and get more clarity about life and your purpose. Meditation can be used for healing mentally and physically, as well as for creating balance in your life.

Many people meditate to give themselves more clarity and personal understanding, and as a result of this clarity, they develop deeper self-awareness. It helps them to get more focused on their passion and purpose and connect with their internal energy and spirit. By doing this, they actually begin to consciously and unconsciously toward fulfillment and achievement.

You may have heard this saying, "Sometimes, you need to slow down to speed up." Meditation allows you to reflect on what is happening in your life and through reflection, you begin to develop answers that you may have always been seeking. Your mind is very powerful. However, it is also very cluttered and filled with tons of information, some useful and some not so useful. It is important to clear your mind and allow yourself to be free of thoughts, free of the clutter. Once you clear your mind, it is open to seeing things from different perspectives and it can make you more focused on your life journey and the approach you will take to get there.

There are many forms of meditation. Deepak Chopra, a spiritual guru, has many spiritual and meditation videos online that you can check out for yourself. Deepak Chopra has an extensive resumé, haven written over 65 books, and a list of clients including celebrities, professional athletes, CEOs, and more. You can find out more about him and his programs on www.chopra.com.

If you do your research, you will find lots of information on meditation. There are also many applications for your mobile devices with guided meditations you can listen to at home or on breaks at work. Regardless of how you practice meditation, it is important to take time out for yourself each and every day to be still, be reflective, and clear your mind. The spiritual and mental benefits that you gain from doing so are amazing. It may be difficult to get started, but once you do you'll likely find that your meditation time is the best time of your day.

I meditate a few times throughout the day. I start my morning with a 20-minute meditation to help me get grounded for the day. Throughout the day, I have moments of deep reflection, sometimes to music, for five to ten minutes at a time. It has given me a deeper connection with myself and who I am. It has strengthened my spirituality and it has made me more aware of my power and the power that exists around me.

The law of attraction states that you attract what you want. This is very fascinating to me and something that I continue to explore. In order to attract what you want, you have to know what you want and believe that you deserve it. This is where most of us are stuck mentally. We either do not know what we truly want in life or we do not believe we deserve it, partly because we do not spend time with ourselves.

Spending time with yourself allows you to get reacquainted with who you are. I believe that throughout the course of our lives, we lose touch with ourselves due to the demands of life. Meditation is time for you. It allows you to deepen your understanding of yourself and the universe. It will provide clarity on where you are going and what you want to attract in life. Take some time for yourself every day and you will be amazed at what opens up for you.

EXERCISE #1: FIVE MINUTE MEDITATION

Take at least a few minutes each day to meditate. Try Deepak Chopra's five-minute morning meditation. Here is what you do:

1. Find a quiet place where you will not be disturbed.
2. Close your eyes and focus on your breathing.
3. Focus on your heart.
4. Ask yourself these four questions; don't worry about answers.

- Who am I?
- What do I want?
- What's my purpose?
- What am I grateful for?

Do this every morning and the answers will come to you. You will get more clarity and self-awareness. If you are new to meditation, this is a great way to start your day. If you already meditate, continue to incorporate it into your daily routine.

PHYSICALLY SPEAKING

Taking care of your mind is important, however, taking care of your health is just as important, if not more so. You need a healthy mind, body, and spirit to live the life you want. Balance is important in order to stay on course. Too often, people focus on one or two of the three, and they become out of sync because they are mentally, spiritually, or physically exhausted. It is important to take care of your health. You need to eat healthier, exercise regularly, and have a healthy state of mind. Taking time for yourself, physically, is just as important as the mental time outs. In order to have a deeper connection with your inner wisdom, you need to create balance in your life. The best course of action you can take is to gain clarity through physical and meditative activities. A great way to combine both is yoga or Tai Chi. Both of these options allow you to relax your mind and concentrate while you are strengthening your body.

HERE ARE SOME OF THE BENEFITS OF LIVING A HEALTHIER LIFESTYLE:

1. Reduce health risks such as heart disease, high blood pressure, stroke, and diabetes.
2. Help to maintain a healthy weight.
3. Help you manage stress.
4. Increase energy levels.
5. Increase self-esteem.

6. Increase focus on other areas of your life.
7. Motivate you to achieve other goals that you set.

It is no secret that there are many benefits to being physically active, yet it is an area where most people struggle. You may be struggling with your weight or health. You may want to lose weight or live healthier, yet you have no desire to go to a gym or participate in physical activity because it is challenging or it may not be enjoyable. Those views have a lot to do with a negative perspective. Yes, it is difficult to lose weight and be physically active, especially if your goal is to shed a lot of pounds from around your waistline. But if we could shift our thinking about physical activity to a more positive track, the physical aspect of going to the gym would be much easier.

If you can learn to shift your perspective and look at what a healthy lifestyle will give you and your loved ones, it may motivate you to be more active. And just like with your other goals, it is more effective to break your goals down into small bite sizes.

Taking one step at a time helps you to see quicker results and keeps you motivated to keep going. Seeing your progress will also help you to shift your perspective from seeing your long-term physical goals as being impossible to actually see them as achievable. Being physically active will give you the energy you need to achieve other goals in your life. It will help you clear your mind and build confidence.

Consider all the benefits of taking time to reflect, meditate, exercise, and live a healthier lifestyle. If you want to change your life and live your greatness, you need to create a mental, physical, and spiritual balance. To move from being stuck in some aspect of your life to having more fulfillment or happiness, you need to put in significant effort. You owe it to yourself to be your best and make your best attempts to change your life. If you are truly committed, then you must commit to taking care of yourself, allowing you to be a better partner, parent, family member, friend, and employee because you are clearer on who you are and the path you are traveling.

WHAT'S ON YOUR PLATE

You are what you eat! Have you heard that saying before? It means that what you put in your body is what your body reacts to and determines your level of health and wellness. It's no secret that if you eat a lot of unhealthy, processed or fast food, your body will react in a negative way. You will gain weight, you will be sluggish, lack energy, and you will struggle to be active. It may also lead to health issues that may become chronic and possibly debilitating or life-threatening. I am talking from experience by the way. I will be completely transparent.

Here goes...I LOVE FOOD! Yup, that's the truth. I like all types of cuisine; food cooked different ways, and yes, some fast food too! Growing up I used to eat everything, partly because my mom couldn't afford super healthy food so my brother, sister, and I ate whatever was on the table. I just grew up loving to eat. It was much easier to lose weight when I was younger because my metabolism was much higher and I was always running around or playing sports. However, as an adult, not so much.

Being an athlete for most of my life, I was always very active. I was playing on various sports teams, exercising regularly, training at the gym, and getting proper rest. I could eat fast food or food that wasn't necessarily healthy without gaining weight. It wasn't until I was older, in my mid-thirties that my lack of healthy eating caught up to me. It was at that time that I gained 40 pounds. That may not seem like much weight to you, or maybe it does, but for me, an athlete, and usually fit, it was a lot of weight. It might as well have been a 100 pound weight gain for me. Having the extra weight made me lack self-confidence. I became sluggish and I lacked energy. I just wasn't myself. I knew I had to do something to change my situation. I started back at the gym and I started to get my strength back, however, I realized I had to change my diet. I made it a point to eat healthy a minimum of 5 days a week. That's right, I love food and I like to eat lots of types of food, but I wanted to be realistic, so I committed to 5 days a week of healthy eating. It changed everything. My confidence came back, I had more energy and I lost the weight.

What I realized is that what you eat is a HUGE part of maintaining

FOURTH HABIT: MIND YOUR FITNESS AND SPIRIT

a healthy lifestyle and weight loss. You can exercise as much as you want but if you are not eating nutritious healthy meals to feed your body, you most likely will not be in optimal health. On your road to greatness, to personal change, you must first take care of your body. Without your health you have nothing and nothing else matters. I know it's difficult to exercise and to eat healthier, however, like anything else in life, you first must start. Start by replacing a few meals each with healthier choices. Next, progress to ensuring that 2 of your 3 or 4 meals each day are healthier and continue to increase the number of healthy meals over time. You owe it to yourself to take care of your body and food is a big part of self-care.

> **TRY THIS**
>
> Do the 5 minute meditation every morning when you wake up
>
> Schedule time in your calendar to exercise weekly. Aim for a minimum of exercising 3 times per week for 20 minutes or more. You can walk, run, bike, do at home workouts, go to the gym, play a sport; do some type of activity each week
>
> Replace 2 meals a day with healthier choices, try it for a week and see how you feel

You can get these downloadable worksheets at
www.YouHaveTheKeysNowDrive.com/resources

CHAPTER 10

FIFTH HABIT: BE OF SERVICE TO OTHERS

> *"Service to others is the rent you pay for your room here on earth."*
>
> —Muhammad Ali

I ONCE met a guy who had what most people would consider a dream job he interviewed celebrities. Not only did he interview them, but he also had exclusive access to them because he worked for various organizations which promoted movies. He loved what he had done. He had done it for more than 10 years and got to meet everyone from Denzel Washington, to Brad Pitt, to Angelina Jolie.

One day he woke up and said he had enough, he wanted a change. He was tired of the late nights, crazy hours and schmoozing. He wanted something else but was unsure of what he wanted. He loved the job but felt that something was missing. He wanted to do something that had meaning and purpose. So, he quit his job and started working for a nonprofit organization. He said it was the best decision he ever made. He loves the work and enjoys giving back and helping others learn and grow. He feels alive again and he has a new-found appreciation for life and for being of service to others.

I truly believe that we are all put on earth to find our true gift and use it to be of service to others. Contributions beyond ourselves give us balance and fulfillment, something even some of the most successful people seek. There comes a point in life when acquiring things and achieving goals isn't enough. That is when most people go on a quest to find out who they really are, what their real purpose is, and how they can be of service to others.

We are here to give. To give love, to give a helping hand, to give knowledge, to give encouragement, to love and to listen. In times of personal or professional struggle, we often focus on ourselves. However, when you give you receive. There is nothing like the feeling of giving someone a gift, something that they absolutely need or want but can't attain themselves. It makes you feel great and happy and distracts you from your own challenges.

What you need to know is that you matter. Your story matters. Your experiences matter. Your gifts and talent matters. There are thousands of people in this world who are waiting for you. They need you to step up and share, help, and guide them. There are so many ways that you can be of service…Maybe you are a great writer - you can help students struggling with writing essays. Or you are great at organizing - you can help single mothers organize their homes. Perhaps you are skilled at financial planning - you could volunteer at a community organization to help families who are struggling financially organize their finances. It is not about being an expert in a field, it is about volunteering and helping others in a way that is true to you. Too often people wait **until** – to give back. They wait **until** they have a certain dollar amount in their bank account. They wait **until** they reach that job title they always wanted. They wait **until** they have the house and the car they wanted. They wait **until** they reach a certain level of success. The people who need your help don't need you to have a certain level of success, they just need YOU. When I speak to youth groups, organizations, community groups, and other audiences, the participants don't care that I haven't achieved everything in life. They are there because they are seeking knowledge, information, and some are on a personal journey to change their lives. For me, it is about adding value to someone's life and that, in turn, adds value to my own. Every time I speak, coach, or write, I learn more about myself. I understand myself and my place in the world more and more.

Something happens to you internally on a spiritual and mental level when you serve others. Even during times when you are struggling or going through difficulties, when you serve others you open the window to gratitude. Helping others is what life is all about. It's about more than building a legacy, it's about humanity. It helps you gain clarity during those moments when you are unclear about the direction of your life.

CLARITY

By serving others and showing empathy and compassion you begin to become clearer about your place in the world and you walk towards finding your true gift. There is something in helping others that unlocks closed doors, allowing us to access clarity in our lives and fulfill our purpose. You begin to explore ways you can serve more, do more, and help more combined with your special talent or gift. As the universe will have it, you get what you give. If you give love, guidance, and support to those who need it most, you will get it all back in return. You will also discover things about yourself that you didn't know before. Serving others gives you the gift of clarity. It could be clarity about your personal development, your health, your career, your relationships, your faith or it could be clarity about your morning ritual, or your life journey. The reason that extremely successful, generous, people give so much is not just because it allows them to help those less fortunate, but it also helps them gain more clarity about who they really are.

Why is this so important? It's important because in life we often get disconnected from our values and passions. We sometimes make decisions that are misaligned with our values and as a result, we lose pieces of who were really are. In the midst of being unclear, sometimes life unravels and we feel lost, stuck or feeling like we are living in a fog. I've felt this way at times. Many of my coaching clients have felt like this, and many of my friends and family have had the same feeling. How do you move past that? How to you get unstuck, come out of the fog, or find your way back to your values, passions and even purpose or true gift? One of the ways is by giving. Giving to others gives to you. It gives you clarity, re-energizes you and helps you re-focus your attention on taking action.

Think about your own life. When was the last time you served others? When was the last time you volunteered your time to work with those most in need? What was happening in your life at the time? How did it make you feel to help? What opened up in your life as a result of serving? These are some things for you to think about.

BUILD YOUR LEGACY

If you were to die today, what would be said and written about you at your funeral? Not next week, not tomorrow, but today? What would be said and written about you? Would you be happy with it?

Those were the questions I asked a group of Finance and Technology professional back in 2016 during a keynote speech. As I looked into the audience I saw looks of shame, others were in deep thought, and others smiled and nodded in agreement. They are bold questions that most people never ask themselves until they are far along in life, have reached certain milestones in their careers or finances, or are facing death. Most people don't think about their legacy because they are too busy living. From struggling to pay bills, stay healthy, raise kids, to their own personal and professional development, most people don't have time to think about their legacy. The thing is we are all building our legacies every day.

Every day you wake up you are affecting the lives of others. Every day you are serving others, your children, your coworkers and customers at your job, friends, family, or places where you give your time or donate your services. It is important to understand this so you can understand that every interaction you have with others contributes to your place in the world. When you make a conscious effort to positively interact with people and to help where and when you can, you not only get that back in return, it is your way of giving to the world.

After that keynote, a few people came up to me and admitted that they would not be happy with what would be said about them today if they were to pass away. One person admitted that he was so focused on his career that his relationship with his wife and kids was suffering and he realized that his family is more important than a job. He said his legacy is raising his children to be who they want to be and to teach them to follow their dreams and serve others. It was a very vulnerable and honest moment for him. He got real with himself about who he is and who he wanted to be, and the person he needed to be for his family. There are a few lessons here, but the biggest lesson is that you were born to serve. You can serve thousands of people or a few people. You can serve strangers in need or family and friends

FIFTH HABIT: BE OF SERVICE TO OTHERS

in need. You are the driver of your destiny and the navigator of your legacy. Be conscious about how you treat others and if you choose to serve more, then reach out and do it. Whether you volunteer at a food bank or soup kitchen, or raise money for a worthy cause, or help out at your church or community centre, take action if that is what you want to do. What's important is to remember that every day you are in service to your family, friends, coworkers, and people in your community. You probably just don't see it that way because you have close relationships with those individuals. However, you are affecting their lives in numerous ways. It is important to be conscious of that. What I am talking about is continuing to expand your impact, to serve individuals outside of your circle.

Being of service is about you getting real with yourself. You must find things that interest you and that are aligned to your values. If you want to donate money to a charity you believe in, then do it. If you want to volunteer with an organization that may have helped you or your family members in the past, go for it. If you want to write a blog and share parenting tips for parents who are having challenges, get posting! Helping others is in a way of helping yourself. You are happier, you feel more loved and needed, you have the ability to change lives and, in the process change your own. Think about how you can be of service to others and put yourself out there and do something. You will be surprised by what it does for you and how great you feel.

> **TRY THIS**
>
> Make a list of ways you can serve others: volunteer, send a cheque, use your skills, mentor someone, anything you can think of. Then decide to take action on at least one thing
>
> After you complete your service, journal about your experience. What happened, who you met, how you felt, the response from those you helped
>
> Continue to be of service and continue to journal, looking back at your journal after 6 months to see what you learn about yourself and your place in the world

You can get these downloadable worksheets at
www.YouHaveTheKeysNowDrive.com/resources

CONCLUSION

"Everyone can rise above their circumstances and achieve success if they are dedicated to and passionate about what they do."

—Nelson Mandela

WHAT CAN I say? I am constantly striving to live my life purpose of helping other people discover and live theirs. Seeing people move from living life according to other people's expectations to transform their lives is a monumental experience. It is amazing to see people who are, in a sense, unchained. I don't mean physically; I am talking about being mentally and spiritually unchained when they understand that they have the ability to have more success, more fulfillment, and a deeper understanding of who they are. You deserve the same.

You have gifts to offer the world. Do not let anyone tell you otherwise. You deserve to live a great life. You can live authentically and become the best version of yourself. If you want it, claim it. I know it is not easy, but most things worth achieving are not easy. Reading this book and doing the work (if you have indeed done it or will do it) may not be easy, but you have made it this far. Taking care of yourself and being authentic and true to who you are is the best gift you can give yourself and your loved ones. You can design the life that you want. You have the ability to accomplish things that you never thought possible. It all begins with changing your habits and taking action.

When you want to move forward in life and live your dreams, you have to believe you deserve it and go after what you want with fierce determination and passion. It is not easy to change your mindset. It is not easy to look at your situation from different perspectives; however, you can do it. You must to take action and do something now.

Those daunting voices of self-doubt and disbelief need to be replaced with positive mantras, a burning desire to succeed, and a plan to achieve your goals. By doing this, you will attract what you want, and be who you want to be.

You have to gravitate toward things that bring you joy and happiness. Connect with people who are positive and supportive, people who make you happy. Take care of yourself mentally, physically, and spiritually. Life is a journey; take time to appreciate it. Connecting with yourself is the most important thing you can do in life.

A friend of mine once told me that she looked at life as if she were on a plane. She said that flight attendants go through their instructions and always say, "In the event of an emergency, oxygen masks will drop down from the ceiling. Place the mask over your nose and mouth and secure tightly. If you are traveling with small children or someone who is unable to place their mask on, place your mask on first and then assist them with theirs." Now, I know you do not want to compare your life to being in a plane where cabin pressure drops and you need oxygen. But the message here is that you must take care of yourself first to be in a better position to assist others. This is true throughout your life. In order to be the best partner, parent, sibling, friend, family member, or colleague, you must be at your best, and that starts with taking care of yourself first.

When you are happy with your work or financial situation, feeling good about your physical and mental health, and experiencing strong relationships with people you care about, you are more likely to be at your best and be living a happier life. When you are living this life, you are giving the universe a gift. That gift is the talent and greatness that you bring to your family, friends, and those around you.

I went from being just another 'underachiever' who was about to become one more negative statistic by going to jail or even dying because of my lifestyle, to a life coach, public speaker, and entrepreneur. Take that all you saboteurs! In all seriousness, as you walk towards your goals and dreams, you are getting closer to discovering your gift. Once you believe in yourself, you can achieve ANYTHING. We all have journeys and stories to tell. Think of your life five years, or ten years ago. You have overcome many challenges and you might still be trying to overcome obstacles as you are reading this book, but your journey continues. You are not done. You can achieve your goals and live a happier life, but you must believe it is possible and be willing to do the work that needs to be done.

Appreciate your journey, both the positivity and success that you have had in your relationships, career, health and finances, and everything else. Bask in the enjoyment of your great achievements, but do not settle. Want more, dream big, and go after your goals and dreams with great determination, not letting the fear of the pursuit get in your way. Also, remember to celebrate your failures. That's right, I said it, celebrate the challenges, unsuccessful goals, the difficult times, and the difficulties that you have faced in life. In all of those situations, you have gained wisdom and strength, and you are still standing. Carry this forward in life. Keep fear close and acknowledge that it is a part of life; however, do not let it stop you from living the life you deserve. You can escape from/ free yourself from the mud and transform your life.

Look at what you have done just in reading this book. If you have read the book from the beginning and completed the activities, let's recap what you have already achieved:

1. You have completed your **Wheel of Life** and **Your Life Vision** exercises to help you get clear on your life vision
2. You have re-discovered who you are and even developed your '**I Am**' **Statement** worksheets
3. You have completed the **Finding Your Passion** and **Purpose** worksheet to help you discover your passions and purpose
4. You developed a **morning ritual**, one of the most powerful sets of habits that will transform your life
5. You got real with yourself about who is really supporting you in your life and completed your **Life Decisions** worksheet
6. You completed the **Simple Goal Plan** and got going on your goals

7. You have identified people to be in your **Life Support Network** to help keep you focused and on track
8. You have explored **meditation** and taking time for yourself
9. You made a commitment to your health and wellness through **exercise** and a **healthy diet**
10. You dug deep into how you can be of service to others and you made a conscious effort to serve others

Congratulations on your success so far. You have come a long way! However, your journey is not over -it's just beginning! Continue on your path to achieve your goals and live your dreams. Whatever you think is possible—is possible. Don't let ANYONE or ANYTHING stop you, including yourself. Instead, replace negative thoughts with positive mantras, visualization, meditation, and positive people who will continue to support you in your journey to have more of what you deserve. If you have not done any of the exercises you can always go back and do them when you are ready. This book is not about checking off a list. I wrote it to help you with your personal development journey, regardless of where you are on that journey. It was designed to help you with your personal change – to unlock your personal power. Remember, if you do only ONE thing different, make sure you create your morning ritual. That is the one thing that will absolutely unlock the personal change you are seeking.

If you have signed up for your book bonuses I will continue to send you life-help tools and resources. I am always learning and growing and sharing what I learn through e-mails, videos, and in the **Driver of Your Destiny** community on Facebook. I hope you have enjoyed your journey so far. I wish you much success, happiness, health, and peace on your quest to living your dreams.

I love this quote by Nelson Mandela:

> *"Everyone can rise above their circumstances and achieve success if they are dedicated to, and passionate about what they do."*

Who better to admire, who better to look to as a role model for achieving the unthinkable, who better to inspire you to live your dreams than

CONCLUSION

Nelson Mandela! He taught us that no dream is impossible. Nothing is out of reach if you are dedicated and passionate about what you do and what you want in life. He was a man who was imprisoned for 27 years on false charges, became President of South Africa, and ended Apartheid. Think about that the next time you think your goals are impossible. You are the driver of your destiny. You are the person who can get out of the passenger seat, kick fear, self-doubt, and other people's opinions out of the driver seat and become the driver of your life; the driver of your destiny. You have everything you need to change your life you just have to get started!

Always remember ... you have the keys, keep driving.

Appreciate and enjoy your journey.

SPECIAL INVITATION FOR YOU

Driver of Your Destiny Community

Readers, fans, and followers of "You Have the Keys, Now Drive" and my work are extraordinary people committed to waking up ready for personal change and ready to unlock their true potential. Knowing that there are many individuals ready to make a shift in their lives that don't have the tools or resources to do so, inspired me to create the Driver of Your Destiny community. The community is a place for you to connect, share ideas, get guidance and support, discuss the book, find accountability partners, and motivate others.

Sign up for the free community on Facebook at www.facebook.com/groups/driverofyourdestiny

Here you will connect with like-minded individuals who are committed to personal change and personal growth. You can share your keys to personal change stories, discuss how you are building your confidence, and share how your new habits are helping you achieve your biggest goals.

I will be moderating the community, regularly checking in and commenting.

I would love to hear from you on social media.

My name is **@iamDannyStone** on Instagram, Twitter, Facebook, Pinterest, and YouTube. Please feel free to comment, like and direct message me. I read every comment and do my absolute best to personally respond. Looking forward to seeing you in the community and on social media!

Go to www.facebook.com/groups/driverofyourdestiny

ABOUT THE AUTHOR

Danny Stone is an Author, Speaker, Coach, Personal Development Teacher, Philanthropist, and Community Servant who has dedicated his life to helping people tap into their personal power by changing their habits. He has helped countless people define what success looks like for them and worked with them to take massive action to get what they want in life. He is a Certified Training and Development Professional that has taught and coached individuals in some of Canada's Top companies.

Having spent years as a career and life coach, Danny has helped hundreds of people find meaningful careers, launch businesses, earn more money, build their confidence and shift their lives in positive ways.

Life wasn't always this fun for Danny. He grew up in a low-income housing community surrounded by drugs, crime, and violence without a father, and he was headed down the wrong path. Many of the people he associated with were in and out of jail and others were killed as a result of the lives they led and the choices they made. Danny decided he didn't want to live a life of crime. Instead, he took action and changed his life for the better. He became a positive influence and mentor in his community working with youth to show them how to walk positive paths.

He is constantly studying and learning about personal development, goal achievement, and success and he is committed to teaching others how to unlock their greatness.

Some of his proudest accomplishments are receiving messages from youth he has mentored and people he grew up with. Danny loves reading messages about how they have changed their lives or stayed on positive paths because of his guidance or mentorship means so much to him. It is difficult to stay focused on becoming your best self in the midst of many setbacks and challenges, however, he believes that ANYONE can realize their potential.

Danny's current mission is to teach people all over the world how to become the drivers of their lives. He currently teaches people personal development and entrepreneurship topics to help build their confidence, change their habits, and unlock more happiness. His other current mission is mentoring youth through various mentorship programs and he continues to donate a percentage of all book sales to youth programs including **Zero Gun Violence Movement** in Toronto, Canada.

He would love to connect with you on social media. He is on the main platforms, Instagram, Facebook, Twitter, under the name @iamDannyStone.

You can also reach Danny on his website www.iamDannyStone.com

HIRE DANNY TO SPEAK!

Book Danny to speak at your next event and he will deliver high energy, inspiring, engaging and entertaining experience. For more than a decade Danny has been lighting up audiences both large and small with his tell-it-like it is, humorous, honest speeches. He is a master at telling stories and has a way of getting the audience, thinking, laughing and energized. With his powerful story of near-death experiences, transforming his life from growing up poor in the inner city to traveling the world, to becoming a lifestyle entrepreneur, he will have audiences ready to take action.

Danny has dedicated his life to helping people unlock their potential and walk towards becoming the best version of themselves. Empowering people to take control of their lives and become drivers of their own destiny is something that he continues to do through his speeches, coaching, book, online community, social media, and TV appearances. If you want a speaker who will inspire your audience, someone with real actionable strategies that produce results, then contact Danny to speak at your next event.

To Learn More Visit www.iamDannyStone.com

www.ingramcontent.com/pod-product-compliance
Lightning Source LLC
Chambersburg PA
CBHW050434010526
44118CB00013B/1525